THE
SOUTHERN WAY
Issue No 9

CONTENTS

© Kevin Robertson (Noodle Books) and the various contributors 2010
ISBN 978-1-906419-28-8
First published in 2010 by Kevin Robertson
under the **NOODLE BOOKS** imprint
PO Box 279
Corhampton
SOUTHAMPTON
SO32 3ZX
www.noodlebooks.co.uk
Printed in England by
Ian Allan Printing Ltd
Hersham, Surrey

Something slightly different on page 4 for this issue: different, that is, to our usual type of illustration this early on. Previously, I have often attempted to include views that might be considered to be 'high-impact' on the early, intro-ductory pages of each SW issue, as witness the strong images that have appeared in the past: fear not, we will revert to them again in future. I like to think that 'SW' has perhaps now found a following among those who would welcome a variation from the norm: not a locomotive nor station, not even a goods yard; instead the sad remains of another brave Bulleid experiment, the sides of a Tavern Car, we know not which one, removed and cast aside ready for dis-posal. The location is the Carriage Works at Eastleigh on 26 August 1950, by which time the initial enthusiasm for the enclosed 'olde-worlde' image Bulleid had created had been replaced by a modern no-nonsense Marylebone Road approach. Ironically, on the same day and close nearby, another of Mr. Bulleid's less than conventional creations, 'Leader', was undergoing dynamometer car trials from the running shed. Putting the steam engine aside though, and returning to the subject of the Tavern Cars, from recent study of the political situation on the Southern Region post-nationalisation, it appears as if BR were distinctly unaware of exactly what Bulleid was creating in these vehicles. The only edict was that all new coaching stock was to be painted in the corporate two-tone 'blood and custard' livery. One cannot dispute that the Tavern Cars complied in this way, although not quite in the manner intended. Seen here is a discarded side from the Restaurant portion, the panelling carefully removed to preserve the coach framework, although the sheets seen here were hardly likely to have much further use. Why did Bulleid behave the way he did is a question that has been asked countless times before. Undoubtedly a genius in many ways, he simply appeared unable to conform to the conventional; you just never knew what he was likely to get up to next. As regards the unconven-tional rolling stock we are referring to, what seems the greatest shame is that whilst seeming to be applauded initially, very soon an amount of 'spin' began to appear, led by certain daily newspapers, which ridiculed the vehicles. This was then taken up by BR as justification for their rebuilding. This also was somewhat strange, since it was freely ad-mitted that the cash takings from the cars was far greater than had been anticipated and remained at a consistently high level: perhaps an early example of the public actually approving of what they had been given, but then being told they could not have what they wanted. Now where have we heard that before?

Editorial Introduction

With this issue, we commence our fourth year of publication and with it our second bumper issue having more than the usual 100 pages. (This also occurred with issue 7).

I have to admit that the intended plan to be strong-willed and keep to the intended page count has clearly failed, simply due to the amount of material I promised I would included in this edition, although it will be back to 100 pages in April.

I am also very conscious that it is important to retain a uniform style and with it thickness, so I do hope the increased content does not appear too unattractive on the bookshelf. Without the need to pay for the cost of a receptionist and a pot-plant we can also keep the cost the same.

It is a pleasure also to include a bit of catching up in this issue, with Part 2 of Lancing and the concluding part of Basingstoke, although I do hope I might be able to persuade the author of the latter, Roger Simmonds, to come out of retirement and dust off his keyboard once again.

What I am very conscious of, and this applies both to submitted material and also the books we publish, is that if an individual has been kind enough to submit material, they have every right to expect it to appear within a realistic timescale. Waiting years is not, in my opinion, an acceptable situation.

As ever though in this issue I have to confess to another imbalance, the South Western and Brighton sides are I hope reasonably well covered, but we are again light on the South Eastern. Vis-a-vis my earlier comment, whilst everything is welcome (and do please keep the articles and photographs / slides coming), if you submit a South Eastern type feature it will probably appear very rapidly. Please don't worry if you have little or even no illustrative material, we may be able to help - or know someone who can.

Around the time of release of the previous issue, I was in correspondence with a regular friend of 'SW' who suggested the idea of a 'SW Annual'. I have to confess I have shied away from such things in the past, basing my reluctance upon the experience of others as well as not wishing to flood the market totally. Southern is still in the ascendancy at present, and whilst I enjoy producing 'SW' it has to be commercially viable. I have no wish to 'kill the goose', so to speak. But do let me have your opinions - please.

Speaking of Annuals, well not quite that exact word, I suppose, our equivalent has to be the various 'Special' issues we produce. I should warn everyone then the intention is for two 'Specials' in 2010, if all goes to plan, both around the same time as Issue 10 in April. 'Wartime Southern Part 2', and 'Southern Colour to the West: Dorset, Somerset, Devon and Cornwall' are the two concerned. Both have only been made possible by submissions from readers, so if you have anything to add please do so, ASAP - please!

Finally my thanks as usual to the team and all who assist in whatever way. This is also the first issue prepared with our replacement computer equipment and from the enlarged office - a colleague commented it would make a superb model railway room: that though is still some way into the future.

Kevin Robertson

Front Cover - *Mainline O2 No. 30225 outside the front of the shed at Eastleigh during its second and final sojourn between March and December 1962. This, together with No. 30199, were the last of the mainland engines in the class left in service, No. 30199 mainly occupied at Redbridge whilst No. 30225 was used for carriage shunting. In the background is the office block, the top floor of which had once been a dormitory. The opportunities for sleep alongside a 24 hour steam shed were clearly not considered at the time the idea of bedrooms was mooted - how long did it remain in that original role? Above is, of course, the water tank and although indistinguishable in the view, complete with its cast plate, 'LSWR Wimbledon Works' (1903 - I think!) The water tank drew its supplies straight from the River Itchen and was of necessity cleaned out on occasions. No doubt certain members of staff also used it for swimming, as occurred at other large similar sites, although we have yet to confirm this relative to Eastleigh. As with the water supplies for the nearly works, fish would invariably be found whenever this cleaning out took place.*

Roger Thornton / KR collection

Rear Cover - *As an accompaniment to the piece on Dorchester that appears in this issue, we felt it appropriate to include this view of the station forecourt. As ever with any view from this period, the eye is instinctively drawn to the motor cars, usually with the comment, "I remember them...", or 'we used to have one of those...'. The green colour scheme, the lamp shades, the barrows, all part of a past life.*

Pages 2 and 3 - *A genuine sop to those who quite rightly have commented there is too little South eastern coverage in 'SW'. Folkestone Harbour Station in September 1921 near to which was the South Pier where the cross-channel business had commenced in 1844. (South Eastern area contributions are always welcome......)*

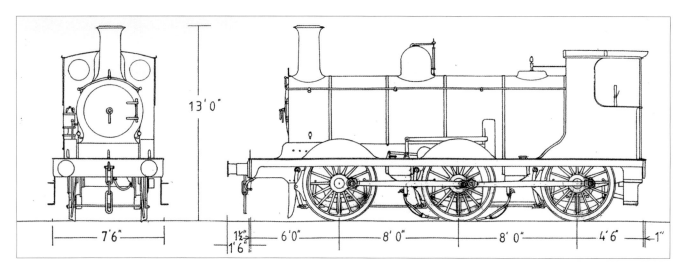

1. C2 Early appearance.

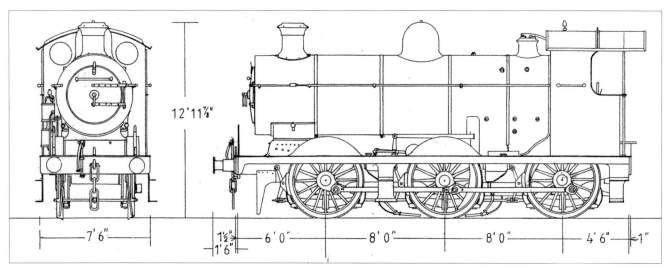

2. C2X Early appearance with early brake modification and altered underframe fittings.

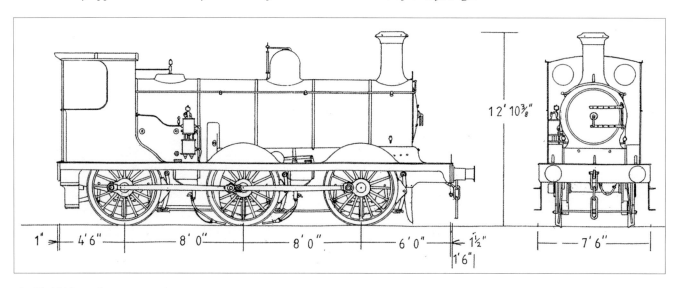

3. C2 1900s with cast-iron chimney.

THE LBSCR C2 and C2X GOODS ENGINES

Gerry Bixley

On his arrival at Brighton from the Midland Railway, Robert Billinton's first new locomotives were his D class (later D3) 0-4-4 tanks which were very similar dimensionally to the Midland's own 0-4-4s. As chief draftsman at Derby, he would have been very familiar with the local products. They shared an 8'0" coupled wheelbase and similar sized boilers and in appearance were a cross between Derby and Brighton characteristics.

For his first goods design Billinton adopted the almost universal 0-6-0 tender, Brighton's C (later C2) class. Great similarities could again be seen in the dimensions of the Brighton and existing Midland engines which shared an 8'0" leading coupled wheelbase and a quite modest boiler, much like the D3 but with a 12" longer firebox. A well-balanced engine resulted with what might be described as delicate proportions.

Brighton works were unable to construct the locomotives which were all built by the Vulcan Foundry, Newton-le-Willows, Lancashire. Unsurprisingly they were always known as VULCANS on their home railway.

Delivery was made as follows:
Nos. 433-444 in 1893
Nos. 445-452 in 1894
Nos. 521-540 in 1900
Nos. 541-545 in 1901
Nos. 546-555 in 1902

As a result of delivery of these 55 engines, a programme of withdrawal of the 20 Stroudley C class was completed by 1904. The Cs had amassed very reasonable mileages in their working lives of around 30

C2 No 537 in experimental livery 1905: original condition.   *G Bixley collection*

7

C2 No 451, circa 1912 with new cast-iron chimney.   *G Bixley collection*

years. This left the 12 Stroudley C1s or "Large Jumbos" which had been built between 1882 and 1887 to cope with the lesser goods workings. These had in fact been slightly larger than the original Cs but were considered Stroudley's least successful design. So Billinton's ideas of replacement by a smaller design are somewhat difficult to understand.

All 55 were similar in appearance when new. Originally, the tenders held only 2,420 gallons, some slightly more at 2,600 gallons, the final increase to 2,985 gallons being achieved by means of a well tank between the leading and centre axle.

Like the D3s, the Billinton chimney design was very shapely and made to blend into the double-jacketed smoke box by careful workmanship. The dome and spring-balance safety valves were carried on the middle ring of the 3-ring boilers. Very few changes took place until Billinton's successor, Douglas E Marsh, provided five new boilers in 1905, similar in size to the originals but with a closed dome on the centre-ring and lock-up safety valves over the firebox.

This proved to be the start of much boiler swapping around the class, as well as the E5 and E6 0-6-2 Tanks which shared a similar boiler requirement, but it was a rather insignificant change compared to the drastic action which was to follow, starting in 1908.

Marsh's contribution to the story is mainly related to his C3 0-6-0 design of which ten engines were

built at Brighton in 1906. These were at first noticeable for their much larger, higher-pitched boilers, larger cabs, shorter chimneys and bigger tenders. Later he introduced a new style of capped chimney, and tastefully shaped safety valve casing which were to become the norm for most Brighton engines through to Southern Railway and British Railways days. Many of the design features appear to have originated with his chief draughtsman, Basil K Field, who had produced somewhat similar designs for the North Staffordshire Railway.

In many ways the C3s appeared more dated than their predecessors, with cramped valve chests, cross-head pumps and outside brake rigging. They also reverted to Stroudley's wheel spacing of 7'9" and 7'6" but the impression given was that of a large and powerful locomotive. Put to work on the heavier duties, it was realised at once that all was not well and no more were built. The boilers and fireboxes were modified but the poor front end did not help and they never appeared to have enough energy for hard work. Marsh was always prepared to experiment, as his trials of 1905 between petrol railcars, steam railcars and 'Terriers' working motor trains proved. He realised that the C2 design was sound and capable of a good day's work on goods or passenger duties if not heavily overloaded and its design remained trouble-free and low maintenance to the end. Abandoning further improvement to the C3s, Marsh decided to try to improve the C2 with his modified C3 boiler design, and as an experiment, he took No 545 into works for overhaul in 1908 and fitted it with the larger boiler. He also had added an extended smoke box, new chimney and much larger cab to complete the transformation. Modifications were made to the under-frame, consisting of new larger cast spring hangers and re-shaped brake hangers retaining the original top pivots, but with the hangers set forward below the brake shoes in an attempt to increase the brake leverage. This modification required the guard irons to the set further forward, as is shown in the illustrations.

When tested, No. 545 did all that had been expected of it, and as a bonus, consumed less coal and water than an unmodified C2 on similar heavy duties. A very purposeful-looking engine which always looked right resulted, and the C3s were quickly allowed to sink into the background and take up lesser duties, many of which were of a lighter nature from Horsham shed. Unsurprisingly, they became known to the men as the "Horsham Goods".

Two further C2s were converted to C2X in 1908, and by September 1911 a total of 20 had been completed. Most appear to have had a further brake modification whereby the top brake pivot point was moved further forward and the hangers were made to a boomerang shape. This necessitated the sandboxes being moved forward by a similar amount. No. 551's brakes appear not to have been so altered, but in later life both No. 551 and No. 545 had the boomerang arrangement.

No. 440 was rebuilt as a C2X in December 1911 but with no alteration to the original springs and suspension. All future rebuilds would be similarly unaltered. It is not clear whether the braking was modified at this time but No. 440 was noted with extended hangers during the Southern Railway period, and of the rebuilds done up to October 1915, all were noted with the same alterations in later years. Photographic evidence shows Nos. 446 and 448 with the original C2 brakes in LBSC days but No. 448 had brakes modified prior to 1923.

In 1912 Lawson Billinton took over running the locomotive department and he had his own ideas about the top feed. He had experimented with his 'K' class moguls, the method used here involving a second, forward, dome with two high-level clack valves attached to the back. Billinton ordered 15 further C3-type boilers with double domes, delivery taking place between 1921 and 1925. The first six new boilers were allocated to existing C2X engines from the first (1908-11) batch of rebuilds.

Billinton continued the rebuilding programme in 1922, adding two further examples before the grouping. The Southern. Railway rebuilt a further eight

C2 as SR No 2435, circa 1933. Fitted with E5 boiler, 2' 9" cast-iron chimney and vacuum ejector. Cab roof also extended.

A B Macleod / G Bixley collection

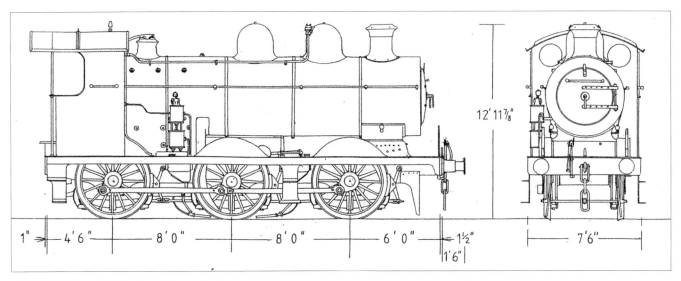

4. *C2X 1920s re-boilering with top-feed.*

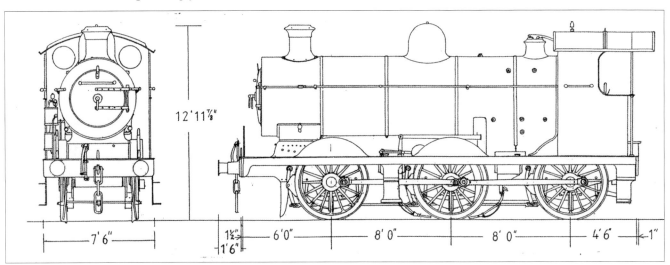

5. *C2X As rebuilt from around 1912 onwards with no underframe alterations.*

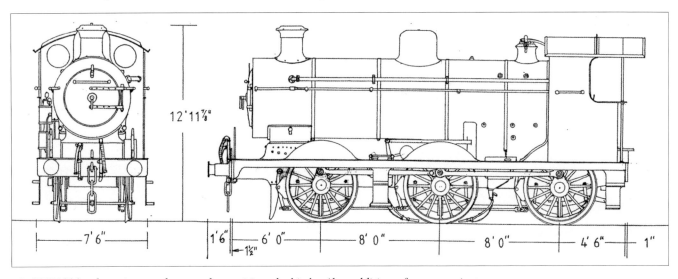

6. *C2X 1920s alterations to dome and repositioned whistle. Also addition of vacuum ejector.*

C2 as SR No. 2527, circa mid-1930s after first Ashford overhaul. Fitted with Ashford buffers.

R K Blencowe collection

C2 as SR No. 2533 at Newhaven, 6th June 1949 when close to withdrawal. Ashford rivets are prominent.

Pamlin Prints / J Scrace collection.

C2X No. 445, a typical early rebuild with new springs and spring hangers, altered brakes, repositioned sandboxes and altered guard-irons   J Scrace collection

in 1924 and two more in 1925, all of the 1922-25 rebuilds using older boilers. Towards the end of the 1920s all the C2s and C2Xs were fitted with vacuum ejectors. As the C3 boiler design was common to C3, B2X, C2X, E5X and E6X, boilers were swapped frequently. Consequently the double dome boilers were to appear on many engines, though they lost their top feed over the first few years, the views of Richard Maunsell favouring side feed arrangements for the type.

Eventually all C3 type boilers had side feed but the second domes were retained. Only ten C2Xs appear never to have been double domed.

While all the development of the C2Xs was taking place, the C2s were relegated to lighter work. They went through various changes to boilers and boiler mountings during the period of Brighton ownership (notably, new cast iron chimneys with caps) but were generally unaltered. From 1924 the C2s' cab roofs were extended backwards and C2s of whatever origin, were gradually fitted with side feed. The number of C2s had somewhat reduced by this time and those remaining were scattered round the system though they did not stray off the then Central Section; whereas the C2Xs which had their domes lowered (flattened) were known to have been used on the Chatham lines and also west of Portsmouth from 1924 onwards.

Overhauls were transferred to Ashford from Brighton in 1930 and taking their responsibility seriously it seems, Ashford commenced to fit various SECR design fittings, probably from condemned locos, to both C2 and C2X locos. These included Ashford injectors (behind the cab steps), tapered or stepped buffer shanks with large head buffers, Ashford flush smoke box doors and other minor fittings. As B2X 4-4-0s were condemned, some of their tenders circulated around the 0-6-0s. Some of the swaps involved the larger 3,112 gallon C3 type. Whatever type of tender, Ashford fitted plates behind the LBSC coal rails with the exception of the back rails. Another noticeable Ashford effect was that the previously smooth, flush riveted Brighton engines gradually became similar to their SECR counterparts with exposed rivet heads. In fairness, it must be said that Brighton sometimes did repairs with exposed rivet heads, for example, after accident repairs to buffer beams. It came as a complete surprise when in 1939 two more C2X were created, followed by a final pair in 1940, all using the existing boiler float. The Second World War must surely have contributed to these rebuilds.

The 1930s saw the footplate steps modified with small side pieces added to the treads to reduce the chance of slipping accidents. The C3 tenders were wider than the C2 variety and their steps had to be inset slightly reducing the overall width from 8'9½" to 8'6". Ashford had not quite finished their 'Southeasternisation' however, and several of the capped C2X chimneys had the cap ground down at the bottom to eliminate the lip so that it resembled one of their local products, as applied to an Ashford C for example. This seems to have been done purely for reasons of appearance. Intending modellers really do need good photographs to model these locos. A final change in the 1950s concerned the tenders. For some reason, the LBSC tanks were removed from a number of under frames and replaced by 3,500 gallon LSWR tanks. These were too long to suit the Brighton frames so were shortened slightly at the front end to fit. The Brighton front plate and brake columns were therefore unaltered. The unaltered tenders had the LBSC tool boxes which had curved tops replaced by SR Pattern flat top examples from the late 1940s. The double dome boilers retained their second domes to the end even though top

C2X No. 545 as the first to be rebuilt in 1908.   *G Bixley collection*

C2X No. 549. A 1912 rebuild with no underframe alterations.   *J Scrace collection*

feed had been removed 30 years before, although one unidentified C2X was photographed with a round plate affixed to the cladding where the second dome would have been.

Withdrawal of the C2s extended from 1935-1950. The more useful C2Xs were withdrawn between 1957 and 1962. One set of C2X tender wheels survived to be re-used for the Bluebell Railway's new-build H2 Atlantic "Beachy Head".

The C2s were originally painted Stroudley goods green lined in black, except for the black smoke box and red buffer beams which were lined black and white. Cabside number plates were oval-shaped brass and buffer beam numerals were gold block. Coupling-rod joints were bright finished. In 1905 three of the class were subject to livery experiments. The standard chosen was overall black with red lining, with LB & SCR on the tenders. This was simplified to LBSC from 1912. A few examples of C2X appeared in umber, lined black and straw, just before the SR take-over in 1923. Before a decision to paint all goods locos black lined green was taken, a few more C2X appeared in umber, such as No. 532 in March 1924. No. 451 was noted in black in April, then No. 523 was noted with green wheels in May - whether it became all green is not known. In August 1924 No. 536 appeared in umber. Later in the 1920s all received SR cabside plates with 'B' prefixed to their numbers, from 1932 this was changed to 2xxx series

numbering. Corresponding numbers were painted on the tender sides under the Southern name.

The buffer beams continued to be numbered, usually with SR "expanded" characters. Gradually in the1930s the green lining disappeared, cabside plates were removed and when repainted this was in block lettering. No C2s survived to be affected by British Railways' lettering and crest ideas, but all C2Xs received BR numbering (some were given the interim s Prefixes for a time e.g. Nos. s2532, s2545 and although all received the lion and wheel crest, not all received the final example of the BR emblem.

Duties:

When the first C2s were built they were at once placed on front line duties, being shedded mainly at New Cross, Battersea and Brighton with odd examples elsewhere. Soon their services were used to and from Newhaven, the second series following a similar pattern. The pattern remained the same for many years. Bradley (Locos of the LBSCR Part II), reports two examples of C2s based on the GWR at Westbourne Park in the early 1900s for working coal trains to Three Bridges. He also reports two C2X and one C2 at Old Oak Common from December 1919 to May 1921, also that C2 No. 521 went to the Highland Railway between June 1919 and January 1920. As the X rebuilds became available they took

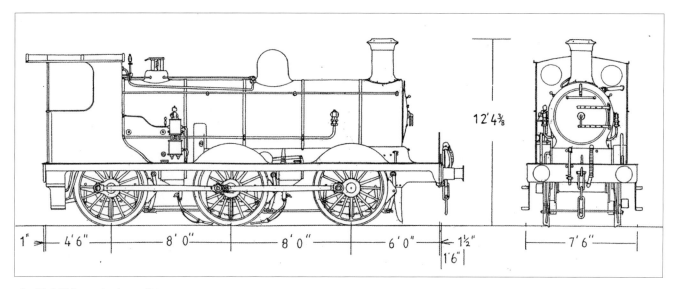

7. C2 1930s typical condition.

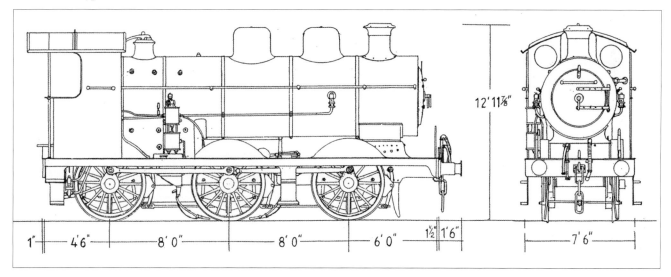

8. C2X 1930s typical double-dome condition.

over the hardest duties with some minor reallocations, so it was possible to see members of both types all over the system, even when the K moguls appeared; for there were many freight and van workings which did not call for the moguls' powers. The C2s in particular were often used for passenger duties such as longer weekend coastal excursions. There were plenty of 0-6-2. tanks for the shorter duties. By 1923 there were 24 remaining as C2, most still at Brighton and the London sheds but with some examples at rural sheds like Tunbridge Wells, Three Bridges and Horsham. The C2X, of which there were then 31, followed a similar pattern; there always seems to have been one at Fratton for instance. Both types seem never to have been in store because of their usefulness. By the early 1930s there were some changes: the S.R. had now fitted vacuum ejectors so passenger duties could be performed with ex-LSWR, ex-SECR and new Southern-built rolling stock.

The Westinghouse air brake was usually maintained but a few C2X had their brake-hoses removed at various times. The air brake turned out to be quite useful when electric stock needed moving about as it would usually be coupled up. Its other great value was for shunting and a C2X could 'stop on a sixpence' if required. During World War II the C2X proved to be extremely useful and were noted on 'foreign' lines special traffic on several occasions. They also strayed to Eastleigh, Tonbridge, Reading and Guildford, the latter being reached on goods workings along the Redhill line and the 'New Line' via Leatherhead and Horsham. A number remained in the London area to the end, some transferred to Norwood Junction. From here their use was on local goods, for example the Wimbledon - West Croydon line. In the country parts of the central section,

C2Xs, accompanied by several Maunsell Q Class 0-6-0s, took over most goods work on the lesser branches e.g. Midhurst, Bluebell Line, Cuckoo Line, Steyning and Guildford branch and after Nationalisation those based at Brighton were often used on lighter passenger duties.

Just for a treat, Horsham men had some experience with 10 - 12 coach through trains from Horsham to Brighton via the Steyning line in the 1950s. These had originated as far away as Reading and came via Guildford, usually brought in by Q1s or 700s.

They became familiar with photographers visiting the Bluebell, for example. The London contingent worked on vans, empty stock and local goods duties to the end. The very last duties were local goods and shunting and engineers' workings from Brighton and Three Bridges. By then diesel shunters were available to carry out their more hum-drum duties.

The C2Xs were remembered for their ease of maintenance, very good braking - the frames never gave trouble - and of course for their handsome appearance.

Three unrebuilt C2s survived the Second World War but all were engaged on very light duties. The pioneer C2X, No. 545 had been a C2X for 53 years, No. 526 for less than 20, for half of which it was double domed. No.535 in 22 years carried four double dome boilers and only one with a single dome.

In preparing this article I have drawn on a number of private records of Brighton Enthusiasts, particularly the late Dick Riley, J N Maskelyne, S D Brailsford and E R Lacey. Also thanks to the works of Don Bradley without whom we would have much less knowledge of Brighton loco history. I must particularly thank Ken Rogers for access to his photos and Alan Blackburn for his photographs of details and measurements of No. 32525 as it awaited the final call in 1962.

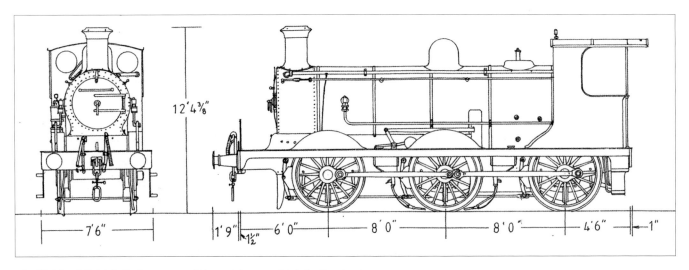

9. C2 Final British Railways condition with some 'Ashfordisation'.

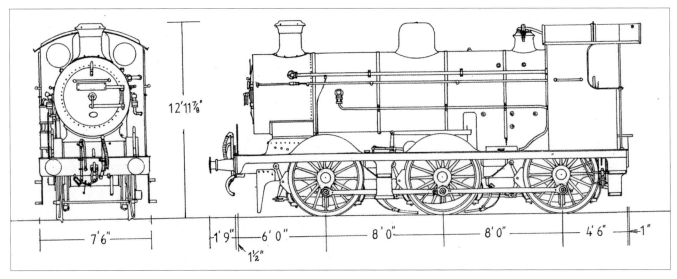

10. C2X British Railways condition with typical 'Ashfordisation'.

C2X No. 448 with pre-1912 livery. Brakes etc unaltered.   *Real Photographs / G Bixley collection*

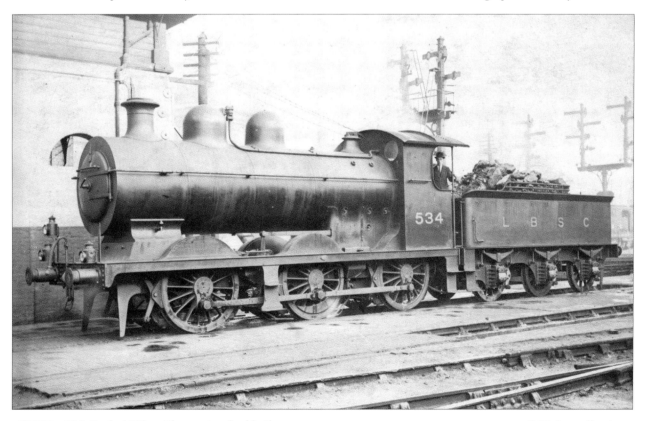

C2X No. 534. Early 1920s with new top-feed boiler.   *G Bixley collection*

Top - C2X No. 554 taken in the 1920s. This shows the top feed.   *G Bixley collection*

Bottom - C2X No. B434, again in the early 1920s and in new SR black livery.   *O J Morris / G Bixley collection*

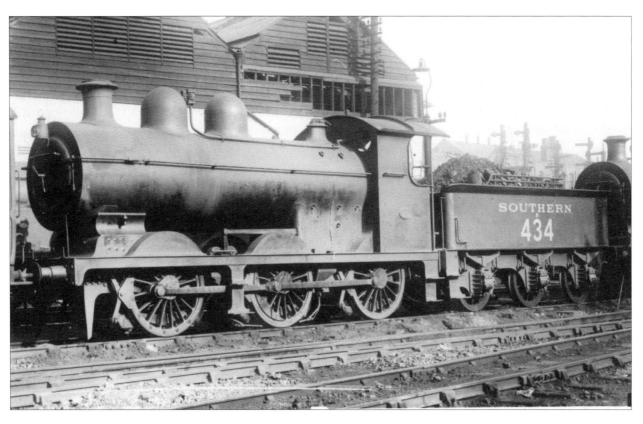

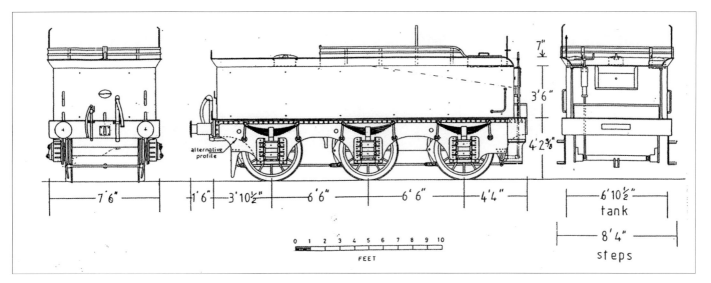

LBSC C2 / C2X

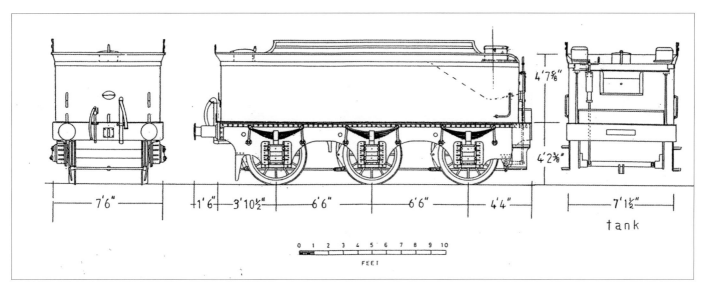

LBSC underframe / LSW tank

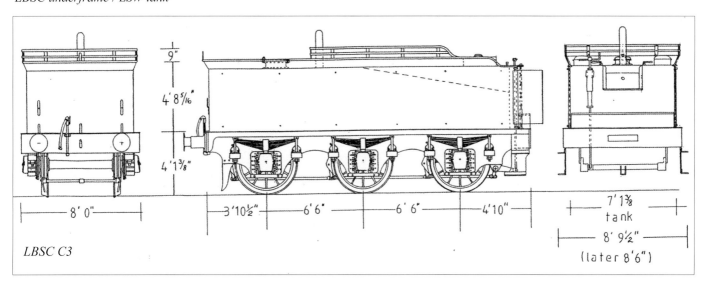

LBSC C3

No	Date Rebuilt	Brakes Modified	Springs / Hangers Modified	Guard Irons Extended	Double Dome Boiler Change	Tender Change	Condemned
					Table 1: C2X Locos 1893 Series		
434	11/1910	Yes	Yes	Yes	3/1921 - 1/1927 : 1/1938 - 6/1941 : 8/1949 - 10/1954		3/1957
437	3/1911	Yes	Yes	Yes	No		6/1959
438	2/1924	No	No	No	7/1938 - 6/1947 : 6/1953 - 12/1958		12/1961
440	12/1911	Yes	No	Yes	9/1952 - 10/1958		10/1958
441	10/1912	Yes	No	Yes	7/1927 - 7/1929	LSW	10/1961
442	6/1922	No	No	No	No	LSW	2/1960
443	10/1924	No	No	No	No		8/1960
444	9/1910	Yes	Yes	Yes	8/1940 - 6/1945 : 3/1957 - 3/1960		3/1960
445	3/1911	Yes	Yes	Yes	No		11/1961
446	6/1912	No	No	No *	7/1945 - 5/1949	C3	10/1960
447	1/1911	Yes	Yes	Yes	6/1928 - 4/1934		2/1960
448	11/1912	No	No	No *	11/1933 - 5/1942		10/1961
449	1/1912	Yes	No	Yes	No		6/1961
450	2/1911	Yes	Yes	Yes	11/1926 - 1/1931 : 6/1944 - 8/1950		10/1961
451	3/1924	No	No	No	1/1928 - 1/1931 : 2/1939 - 2/1944 : 3/1950 - 8/1952	LSW	11/1961

Table 2: C2 0-6-0s not rebuilt, remaining as class C2 until withdrawn

No	Built	Condemned
433	1893	11/1936
435	1893	5/1948
436	1893	1/1950
439	1893	4/1937
452	1894	10/1935
530	1900	10/1935
531	1900	3/1936
533	1900	2/1950
542	1901	1/1937
555	1902	12/1937

Notes to Table 1 -

* 446 and 448 had brakes altered and guard-irons extended much later in life. Exact dates unknown.

LSW - Original LBSCR tender underframe was fitted with LSWR tender tank, 1952 onwards.

C3 - C3 tender (complete) attached to these engines after 1931.

Further tabular information and a Photographic Supplement to the C2X class will appear in 'Southern Way' No 10.

Top - C2X No. B438, seen in early 1920s SR black and clearly lined in green.   *H Gordon Tidy / G Bixley collection*
Bottom - C2X No. 2448 post 1931. Domes reduced in height, Ashford smokebox door fitted together with Ashford buffers. Whistle now on safety-valve casing. Note brakes altered since earlier view on Page 17.   *G Bixley collection*

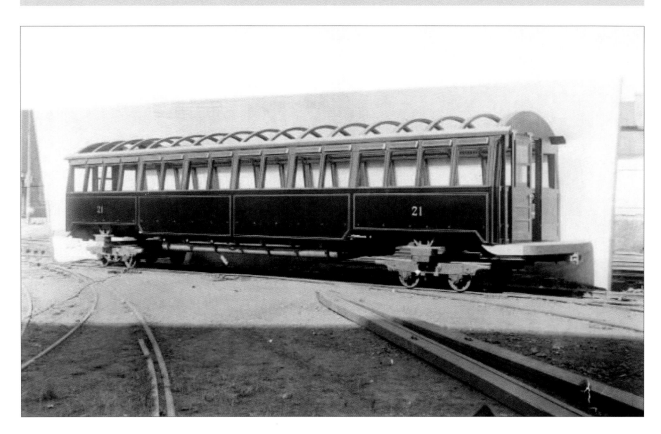

Opened from 8 August 1898, the 'Waterloo & City Electric Railway' was a separate company although backed by the LSWR, who operated the line from the outset, in return for 55% of gross receipts. It was absorbed into the LSWR from 1 January 1907.

Electrified from the outset, the original rolling stock had been in two forms. Firstly, five 4-car sets from Jackson & Sharp of Wilmington, Delaware (later increased to five car sets), and then shortly after opening, five single cars were obtained from Messrs Dick Kerr of Preston. The latter were intended for use off-peak and remained in use for a time post-1940. In addition there were two spare motor coaches and one spare trailer coach. (Current collection was originally from a centrally placed live rail, but this was altered to conventional SR contact on a conductor rail outside of the running rails. This change is reported as having taken place consequent upon the provision of the new rolling stock. At that time it was also reported the original single cars were retained in use for a period, so no doubt both systems operated 'side by side' for a time.) The American-built vehicles were shipped to England and assembled at Eastleigh, being fitted with electrical gear supplied by Siemens of Stafford.

The original stock depicted lasted for over 40 years, by which time it had become the subject of the 'Waterloo and City protest Committee' who challenged the Chairman of the SR, Rob Holland-Martin, over its age, poor ride quality and the general operation of the line responded that "...the line had opened so early it had not had the benefit of other's experience'. To be fair many of the complaints raised were indeed justified. The system then still operated on the principle that tickets would be issued on and also collected on the trains themselves, whilst the ride was certainly harsh and noisy. Improvements though were promised by the SR in respect of new rolling stock, ticket collection to be concentrated at either end of the line and improvements to operation by upgrading the signalling, (the signalling was still as had been installed years earlier, Sykes 'Lock-and Block' with electrically lit semaphore arms at both termini and what was described by B W Anwell in 1940 as. "..a crude type of colour-light signal half way through the tunnel); welded rail joints were also to be provided. All of these though would take time and it was not until early November 1940 that the new stock, designed by Bulleid and having air-operated sliding doors, was ready to go into service. Conflicting reports from 1940 state that the service was suspended for either three or five days to allow the changeover of stock and possible other alterations to take place. Other work was undertaken outside of the times of normal services.

Meanwhile passengers might well have been aghast at the sight of one of the replacement 5-car sets which made a proving run on the main line to Brighton. (Shades perhaps of similar things to come vis-à-vis the movement of former underground stock for the Isle of Wight a quarter of a century later.)

Opposite top - *In the manufacturers yards at Wilmington, Delaware, trailer No 21 is seen, on what are clearly accommodation bogies allowing the vehicle to be moved outside for the benefit of the photographer. This was no doubt a view taken in the course of construction as the roof has still to be added. The extra large sheet of timber was a variation in removing the background, an alternative to the 'painting-out' process adopted, but was surely extremely difficult to move as it is clearly only a temporary feature at that location.*

Opposite bottom - *On the surface, stored and pending disposal. The location is believed to be Horley where the redundant stock remained for some time. The original livery of the trains had been dark brown, later altered to SR green with full lining out and in their final days, plain green. Unusually red was used for the colour of both the headlight and tail-lamp. At peak times, all five 5-car sets operated at 3-minute headway, the labour intensive nature of the operating such that a conductor was provided in each car to issue bell-punch type tickets. (Two conductors travelled on the single cars during off-peak times but still at a 5-10 minute interval working.) The journey time was 5½-6½ minutes*

although it could take 10-12 minutes to exit the station at the end of the journey through the subway then provided. Improvements in these areas did not finally occur until 1960. The power cars were numbered 1 - 12 and the trailers 21 - 36. Sets were identified by a letter, and comprised (in early 1940) the following, Set A: 10,21,22,23,9, Set B: 8,24,25,26,5, Set C: 6,27,28,29,12, Set D: 4,31,32,33,2, Set E: 3,34, 35,36,11. At the time the spare vehicles were thus Nos. 1,7,30. The single units cars were numbered 13 - 17.

Right - *Test run of a new train from London to Brighton passing Keymer Junction.*

A further selection of historic material on 'The Drain' will follow later.

Single Car No 17, seen at Waterloo. There would appear to be visual similarity between this and the American built vehicles. The driving cab only occupied the left hand end of the single cars so affording maximum passenger accomodation.

Opposite top - Control of the original trains by the driver was by means of the large wheel seen which operated contact segments through reduction gearing meaning it had to be rotated several times to travel from 'off' to 'full'. An overrun switch on the trains was trapped by a treadle at either end and could be reset through a system of ropes and pulleys in the cab. A quirk was that although Westinghouse air-brakes were fitted, there was no motor compressor on the train and instead the air reservoirs were recharged from a stationary supply at Waterloo. **Opposite bottom** - Inside a single unit car. On the American built stock, moquette was only provided in the very last days, covering what was a very thin layer of felt over the original wooden slatted seats. It is not clear if the single cars were similarly equipped at the outset. **Bottom** - A train of 1898 stock waiting to come away from the hoist which was the only means of raising and lowering stock, there being no physical connection with any other tube line. The 'M7' is able to draw the stock as the latter was fitted with traditional buffing and drawing gear, although this did not apply to the new stock alongside. The hoist is seen in its original position on the west side of the station and where it remained until the 1980s and the rebuilding of this side of Waterloo for 'Eurostar' operation. A replacement hoist has since been provided on the east side of the station. The new stock on the left was painted in the then latest 'light' shade of SR green with aluminium doors and ends. Pneumatic doors replaced the barriers fitted to the older stock. The new vehicles were also considerably more powerful having motors totalling 760 hp per new five coach train compared with 240 hp previously. It was into this shaft used to raise and lower the Waterloo & City Line stock, that 'M7' No. 672 fell on 13 April 1948 whilst engaged in shunting operations. The engine was little damaged, landing wheels uppermost, but its position meant recovery was deemed impossible and it was dismantled on the spot, various parts being sent in a succession of open wagons to Eastleigh for re-use.

Above - 0-6-0ST 'Bembridge' at the station of the same name.
Below - IOW Rly. 2-4-0 'Ventnor'. Photographed at Shanklin.

Above - IOW Central Rly. No 10 (ex LBSCR No 69), at Horringford.
Below - IOW Central coach No 7 stabled on the Bembridge branch.

All the views were taken circa 1908 and from the collection of V B Orchard having been taken by his Grandfather, G H Read.

Again taken by G H Read from V B Orchard collection.
Above - *Adams '460' class 4-4-0 No 526 is recorded at Queens Town Road on the Nine Elms Good Line.*
Below - *An Easter Excursion train loading at Raynes Park Down Local platform.*

BIDEFORD BRIDGE WIDENING

The bridge over the Barnstaple Road at Bideford in the course of widening sometime in the period 1926 - 1935. The wide timescale assessed from the attire of those visible and the fact that there was shipping laid up in the Torridge at that time. The original structure here was originally a brick arch, and is seen being widened by the addition of an extra span of steel girders. The view is in the Up direction, towards Barnstaple, with, on the left, Bideford Goods Station at Cross Parks, the original broad gauge terminus of the line from Barnstaple. When the Torrington Extension Railway was opened in 1872, a new station was built a little further along the line, opposite the long bridge over the river. The old terminus then became the goods station and it is this that is seen in the photo. According to John Nicholas ('Lines to Torrington' - OPC), the crane in the yard is of 7½ tons capacity. The small signal box can also be seen. Clearly a railway steam crane is in use lifting the new girders, so it is reasonable to assume this was an 'in house' operation with company staff busy offloading cross girders on to the main beam prior to installation. Some are already in place and it may be that the one 'hooked up' at the moment, is about to be lifted into place below the chap on the right. A ladder is just visible to the right of the bowler-hatted gent on the left; one assumes he is the foreman. The crane train is visible standing on the main line, but unfortunately the locomotive cannot be identified. The operation has also attracted a keen audience of locals, so perhaps this was a Sunday occupation. The positioning of this station was highly inconvenient for the people of Bideford, being on the wrong side of the river and some distance from the end of the bridge. The 'new' station at the end of the bridge was little better placed.

The two modern photographs below, show the situation in 2008, with what is now the 'Tarka Trail' running underneath a wide expanse of roadway.

Rod Garner

Above - *The buildings provided consequent to the early 20th century rebuilding of the station still survive basically intact. The entrance at a lower level to the platforms. The then standard informative departure boards will be noted.*
Below - *'S15' No. 30502 leaves the up yard, eastbound, with what appears to be a long train of empties. The fireman will be noted watching for an confirmation from the guard that the train is complete.*

BASINGSTOKE Part 3

Post-War and Beyond

Roger Simmonds

The exigencies of war, although mainly felt in terms of the condition of hard-pressed rolling stock, could also be seen in the general state of the building fabric of the nation's railway stations. Basingstoke was no exception, and the LSWR Engineer reported in a letter of the 20th September 1917 that the station premises were in urgent need of painting and renovation. Tenders for this work were invited, Messrs. Musselwhite & Son being successful at a price of £1,222.

Following the railway Grouping under the 1921 Act, the newly-formed Southern Railway undertook some improvement work in the Basingstoke area over the next decade, this mainly taking the form of signalling rationalisation. The first action was to remove Battledown intermediate signal box (in September 1924), which had in fact been closed for 'a number of years' - its close proximity to Worting Junction and Wootton no doubt reducing its usefulness. The cost of removal was estimated at £166, with the value of recovered materials stated as £131. The saving in maintenance was quoted as £36 p.a.

A major signalling modification was effected on 2nd February 1930, when block telegraph working was dispensed with on all running lines between Woking and Basingstoke. Signals were controlled by track circuits, with indications being given automatically as trains passed on to and off each track circuit concerned. On 21st February 1935, it was reported that illuminated signs in connection with the automatic signals were to be installed at an estimated cost of £10,000 (this included a similar provision on the ex-LBSCR metals). The introduction of automatic signalling enabled the closure of the numerous intermediate boxes along the line.

An approach by Steventon Manor Estate in 1929 for a siding to be provided met with success when the SR agreed, in April of that year, to lay in a siding to accommodate 16 wagons, at an estimated cost of £606; and this was brought into use on the 15th October. The agreement with the owners required them to pay £75 p.a. rental for 21 years, whilst the anticipated traffic volume was hoped to be in the region of 3,000 tons p.a.

However, it seems that it was not a success, as the siding soon fell out of use, and was removed in October 1936.

ANOTHER CHAPTER OF INCIDENTS

Some further occurrences of note in the station area during the 1920s are recorded by the SR Minute books:

18th September 1922 - At 8.15 pm, a platform trolley loaded with six milk churns fell from No. 3 platform on to the Up Through line just before the 5.20 pm Weymouth to Waterloo train was due to pass. The trolley and five churns were removed in time, but the sixth churn was struck by the train engine, damaging the front step. It was stated that Porter Hasler had lost control whilst wheeling the trolley along the platform. The condition of the platform was later blamed.

18th November 1924 - At 2.06 am, the 12.15 am goods from Eastleigh passed the Up Local home signal and collided with the 11.35 pm ex-Southampton train. The engine derailed and several wagons fell over. The driver was suspended for six days, and reduced to shunting duties for six months. The weather was stated to be very foggy at the time of the incident.

3rd October 1925 - A collision occurred between two goods trains at 5.12 am. One train had drawn forward to take water, whilst the other was involved in shunting behind it. Having taken on water, the driver then misread a signal, and set back. Five wagons were derailed in the subsequent accident, blocking the Up Local and Up Through lines.

THE GWR STATION CLOSES

On 1st January 1932, the Great Western passenger station closed, all facilities being transferred to the SR station. Trains from Reading terminating at Basingstoke used the bay which formed an island platform with the SR No 4 platform; the bay was now designated as No 5 platform. To improve access, the gates and iron fencing between the SR and GWR stations were altered in August 1932.

The wooden overall roof was removed, although the wooden station building and water tank

Previous instalments in this series appeared in Issues Nos 3 and 5 of THE SOUTHERN WAY

'Jack', the Basingstoke dog collecting on behalf of the Southern Railways children's home at Woking. (A history of the home at Woking featured in Issue No 8. One of these collecting dogs survives in its 'static' role in the 21st century, still collecting for the same charity. It was recently sent away for 'overhaul' but has since returned to its present home on the Bluebell railway.)

were retained, the former as staff accommodation. Goods traffic between the two systems was still heavy (mostly in the Down direction), with wagon transfers to the SR yard for marshalling into workings for Southampton and Portsmouth. Local traffic was dealt with in the GW yard, including coal and livestock, especially cattle.

A former GW Station Master recalls that an added problem for the staff in handling transfer traffic concerned the different loading height restrictions of the GWR and SR. The latter's dimension was two inches lower, and the GW men were frequently faced with re-loading wagons from the GW system to meet the SR gauge before transfer could take place.

The same year saw the end for the light railway to Alton, which had struggled on manfully with dwindling receipts since the re-inception of services in 1924; the last passenger train ran on 12th September. Goods services continued from Basingstoke to Bentworth & Lasham until 1936, the line being severed beyond that point in the intervening period. At the Basingstoke end, part of the line was retained for access to Messrs. Thornycroft's siding, which remained in use until 1967.

AT WAR AGAIN

As with the rest of the railway network of Britain, the outbreak of World War II had an immediate effect on traffic through Basingstoke. On 11th September 1939, an emergency timetable was introduced, which severely reduced the number of ordinary services, and imposed an overall speed limit of 45mph on those remaining. Naturally, this led to a considerable deterioration in the quality of services, with late running and overcrowding rapidly becoming the norm. These restrictions were eased somewhat from October, although the transport requirements of the war caused limitations on normal services throughout the conflict. Although many of the supply trains from the north took the form of direct services to the ports, a great volume of military traffic was held and re-marshalled in the West yard. This soon became choked with rolling stock, and a series of improvements aimed at increasing accommodation was undertaken, paid for by the Government.

Three additional sidings in the Up yard were provided in July 1940 for an estimated cost of £2,382. These were followed in September by provision for further siding accommodation by undertaking the necessary earthworks for the 'future needs of wartime traffic'. The cost for this work was stated as £7,532 (excluding some additional land, £360, paid for by the SR). On 26th March 1941, it was agreed that traffic had reached the point where this facility should be brought into use. Four marshalling sidings and a shunting neck were laid in, together with a facing connection from the Up Local line to the Up siding, at an estimated cost of £11,194.

About the same time, a salvage dump was established alongside the branch to Park Prewett Hospital. This consisted of an area of some 53 acres (now occupied by the Ring Road) which was fed by sidings off both the main line and Up West Yard. Other improvements for the military in the West yard during 1941/2 consisted of:

12th June 1941 - Facilities for engines taking water. Estimated cost £200.

2nd July 1941 - Provision of cabin in Up yard, for shunters.

29th January 1942 - Provision of Up goods reception road, 1,223 yards long, with facing connection from Up local line. Cost estimated at £9,502 (exclusive of additional land required, at £142 10s).

20th February 1942 - Proposed storeroom and lobby for carriage and wagon examiners in Up West yard.

25th June 1942 - Provision of loud speaker equipment at an estimated cost of £200. (Presumably this was to aid shunting operations, and were hand-held loud-hailers).

22nd January 1943 - Lavatory facilities for shunting staff, at an estimated cost of £97.

To facilitate the handling of heavy military equipment, the cattle pens were removed from the Down East yard loading dock in October 1942. The replacement pens (east of the original ones) were temporarily removed, and the dock was resurfaced in May 1944 with concrete slabs at an estimated cost of

£420. This was presumably to enable tanks and heavy vehicles to be dealt with.

Some improvements were also to be made to the locomotive facilities when, on 26th March 1941, it was reported that the existing engine turntable was in a bad condition and was to be replaced by a redundant unit from Burnaby Road, Portsmouth. The cost of this was estimated at £2,100 which included the lengthening of the latter to 70 feet. The turntable was installed on 29th October 1942 along with other unspecified 'improvements' at a total estimated cost of £18,250, recoverable from the War Department. A plan (dated April 1943) shows a proposal to replace the second-hand turntable with a new one from Ransome & Rapier Ltd of Ipswich; this unit was to be the same size, but with a vacuum engine in addition to the normal hand gear, so perhaps the 1942 installation was not entirely successful. Coaling facilities were also improved in March 1943, when a new coal plant was brought into use. This had required the purchase of additional land, made in December 1942. To ease the pressure on the limited facilities for engine crews, which were under great strain owing to the volume of wartime traffic, some additional messing accommodation was provided at the London end of the down platform. This was brought into use sometime after September 1941. Finally, approval was given on 14th October 1946 to provide additional staff cycle storage accommodation, and improved canteen facilities for engine crews.

By comparison, little was expended on the Great Western side. The only facility of note recorded by the Minute Books was the provision of an additional siding close to the engine shed for use as a wagon spur

in connection with locomotive coaling. This was installed in December 1941 at an estimated cost of £365.

THE END OF AN ERA

The years following the German surrender in 1945 were to see a period of rationalisation of facilities, especially after the Nationalisation Act was put into force. Seemingly, almost as a final act of independence, the GWR undertook to repaint the old wooden station buildings in 1947, by then long out of use for the public.

From November 1950, the ex-Great Western engine shed was officially closed, most of the remaining engine crews transferring to the Southern Region shed. A few men remained defiant, however, and refused to move across to the 'old enemy'. One of these men, Sid King, left the railway and exchanged firing locomotives to tending the boilers at Park Prewett Hospital. The engine shed road remained in use, and was used to store wagons. However, on 16th June 1951, and probably due to the poor state of the track, some wagons were derailed at the east end of the shed in a shunting move; shortly after this incident, the track was removed.

Regional boundary changes in 1950 resulted in the former Western Region metals from Basingstoke to Southcote Junction being transferred to the Southern Region. At the same time, the ex-GWR signal box was renamed Basingstoke 'C', remaining in use until the signalling rationalisation of 1966.

The signalling changes referred to also saw the end of the pneumatic system of operation from Woking to Basingstoke, which had given such good service over the years. Who could forget that gentle hiss, rather like an asthmatic old man, just before the arm dropped to the

SR and GWR stations side by side at Basingstoke. The GWR accommodation retained its overall roof until closed at the beginning of 1932. The width of the platform also a throw back to the days of the broad-gauge. At this stage some goods trains were marshalled in the dead-end platform road. The loading dock still witnessed some 50-60 cattle wagons handled daily, which were brought across in batches. Former GWR employee, Ted Carpenter recalls that it was only cattle and not sheep or horses that were dealt with in this way.

'M7' No. 35 outside the three-road shed at Basingstoke.

Former LNER 4-4-2, No. 251 attracting admiring glances as an unusual visitor to Basingstoke on 12 September 1954. The occasion was a special run in connection with the Farnborough Air Show, the train see here at Basingstoke up platform with the Atlantic double–heading D11 class ex GCR 'Director' No. 62663, 'Prince Albert'. (The special had originated from Leeds and Retford and was organised by No. 18 Group, Royal Observer Corps. No 251 ran several specials in 1953/54 but because she had been fitted with a superheated boiler minus its superheater, the engine would not steam properly. Hence the assisting engine. In the previous year the regular assisting engine was a small Atlantic No. 990.)

More normal working, 'N15' No 30772 'Sir Percivale' in the opposite platform to where the preceding view was taken. To the right the changes that have taken place to the former GWR station are visible. November 1957.

Tony Molyneaux - KR Collection.

'off' position.

The sad occasion of the last steam-hauled working through Basingstoke was witnessed on 9th July 1967 as the transition to electric traction on the Waterloo and Bournemouth services became complete. The ex-SR engine shed was closed, and eventually demolished in 1969. The goods shed, although closed for its original purpose in 1968, did not succumb to the bulldozer, but was retained as a parcels shed, whilst the former yard sidings were adopted for use as storage for rolling stock awaiting disposal. The former Great Western scene has been all but obliterated, although the 1904 stables (at the end of the yard) still resolutely stand amongst the modern 'decay', now thankfully a listed building.

ACKNOWLEDGEMENTS

One is always reliant upon the assistance and co-operation of good friends, colleagues and official custodians of the nation's railway heritage in the preparation of an account. This article is no exception to that well-worn rule. First and foremost I must thank John Fairman, whose intimate knowledge and eye for detail in matters of the "Sou'-Western" deserve higher acclaim, not least for gently abating the exuberant tendencies of the author, and for unbounding hospitality. Reg Randell, the cornerstone of many Southern accounts, also deserves a special mention for turning up the unexpected, and as usual going out of his way to help. Gratitude must also be expressed to Kevin Robertson, a long-standing friend whose ability to winkle out the obscure once again did not fail.

Warmest thanks must also be put on record to the following individuals and organisations: Arthur Attwood; *Basingstoke Gazette*; British Railways Southern and Western Regions; Ted Carpenter, Richard Casserley; H. C. Casserley; Brian Davis; Jack Davis; *Hampshire Chronicle*; Hampshire County Library, particularly Phillipa Stevens; Hampshire County Museum Service, particularly Jan Grant; Phillip Kelley; Sid King; Lens of Sutton; National Railway Museum; the Public Record Office – nowadays known as the National Archive, Kew; George Reeve; lastly Gerry Beale for suggesting it in the first place.

APPENDIX

PNEUMATIC SIGNALLING AT BASINGSTOKE

Discussions relating to trials of low pressure pneumatic signalling on the LSWR system are first reported in 1900, following consultations with the British Pneumatic Railway Signalling Company. In November of that year, the LSWR Directors deferred approval for a trial at Basingstoke, preferring to test the system first at a less important locality. Eventually, Grateley (between Andover and Salisbury) was chosen, and pneumatic

An slightly unusual resident at Basingstoke, in the form of 'E5' No. 32590 seen in company with the former GWR yard shunters truck. The view was taken between April and August 1951, during which time the engine was allocated to the shed for station pilot and carriage shunting duties. This was the first of the class to be seen at Basingstoke, although six others followed up to January 1956. They were reported as popular with crews due to their well protected cab.

John Davenport

signalling was installed during the summer of 1901. The system, developed in the United States by F. L. Dodgson, had been in use since about 1898 in that country. John O'Donnell had managed to secure the British rights to manufacture the system, and formed the BPRS Company at Chippenham. The essential features of the system are that:

1. No force is required, as the power is based on air pressure.

2. Movement of signals and points is by pressure at 15 lbs per square inch.

3. Except when moving signals and points, all pipes conveying air are subject to atmospheric pressure only.

4. The final part of the lever stroke is automatic.

5. Air pressure is supplied from a compressor, located in a power house.

6. Pressure in the pipes laid to the required location can be maintained at only 7 lbs per square inch. This is made possible as the air in the pipe only has to overcome distance, and not resistance. At this pressure it is sufficient to open a valve which allows the required pressure of 15 lbs per square inch to operate signals and points.

7. Points and signals can be worked at greater distances, thus in large installations economies are possible, with fewer signal boxes.

The LSWR were evidently pleased with the success of the Grateley trial, and were discussing further installations with the BPRS Company over the next few

20th April 1962 and No. 35028 'Clan Line' has charge of the 1.30 pm Waterloo - Bournemouth West train complete with Restaurant Car facilities. This particular working was undertaken at a somewhat leisurely pace - perhaps so as to allow potential diners to partake of refreshment without fear of disturbance. Whatever, it meant an average of just 50 mph to Basingstoke which was reached in 57 minutes from London, the complete journey taking 2hrs 50 minutes. The service is seen having just left the station and passing the engine shed: the next stop was Winchester City.

Tony Molyneaux - KR Collection.

months. These discussions led to an offer by the signalling company in December 1901 to equip the section of main line from Woking to Basingstoke for £70,000. This was accepted by the LSWR, subject to the contractual agreements, and also on the basis that the BPRS Company should maintain their system for one year. A further condition was that the Board of Trade would have no objection.

Work was started by the signalling contractors at the Woking end in 1902, progressing through to Barton Mill by early 1903. Power was supplied from a main air-compressing plant at Fleet, where an engine capable of 125hp (assisted by an automatic electrically-worked compressor which came into operation when the steam plant failed to supply sufficient air at the required pressure) was sited. In addition, auxiliary power houses were constructed at Basingstoke and Fleet, each housing two boilers. These were ordered from Messrs. Marshall & Sons of Gainsborough on 21st January 1903 viz. Two power houses £1,500, Four boilers £1,360, Fittings £140,Total Cost £3,000.

In June 1904, the LSWR informed the BOT of its intent to bring the pneumatic signalling arrangements into use between Winchfield and Barton Mill; preliminary inspection of the mechanical interlocking was therefore requested before the new system was completed. Major Pringle duly obliged on 10th June, finding little of any substance to report on, save the fitting of bars to points (Nos 31, 32, 33) at Winchfield, and points (Nos. 28, 29, 30) at Hook.

The Board were notified in October that the Works had been completed, and Major Pringle reappeared on 16th December 1904 to carry out a final inspection. Pringle commented on the rearrangements to the siding connections at Barton Mill since his previous visit, and referred to the signal box containing a frame of 20 levers (with 4 spare). This probably indicates a replacement frame, as in June (some six months earlier) he recorded a 32-lever frame (with 11 spare). A separate contract for installing the system at Basingstoke station was approved by the LSWR in May 1904, at an estimated cost of £13,852. This contract was signed on 29th September with the work to be completed in 20 weeks from that date.

Provisional sanction for this work, along with the other reconstruction work, was sought from the Board of Trade in a letter of 27th April 1904; Major Pringle duly obliged on the 2nd May. The LSWR wrote again on 19th January 1906 informing the Board of their wish for a preliminary inspection of the new signalling work not yet completed. Major Pringle undertook this on 26th January. In his report, he refers to the interlocking in both of the new signal boxes (known as West and East), requiring some minor changes in both cases: East Box (60 Levers, 15 spare) - No. 21 Signal to be made to apply to No. 1 Siding only, and to lock No. 19 Points. West Box (68 Levers, 13 spare) - No. 54 release lever to lock No. 44 Points both ways.

He further stated: *"as the pneumatic system is not yet in use and the track and section indicators are not yet provided in the signal boxes, I was unable to see the working of the points and signals."* These two new boxes replaced three existing cabins. The fact that the completion of the signalling installation was delayed by some months may have arisen owing to the complexity of the project. The *South-Western Gazette* records in August 1907: "The complete working of Basingstoke station and yard is by pneumatic power and amongst the most difficult accomplished by the Pneumatic Signalling Company."

Few problems were experienced with the pneumatic signalling equipment; the system operated satisfactorily until converted to electro-pneumatic operation shortly before the outbreak of war in 1914. This in turn survived until the advent of MAS in 1966.

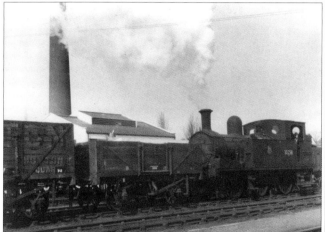

Top left - *'G6' 30258 shunting at Basingstoke in 1951. This particular engine survived until 1961. This was the usual motive power for the trips over the Park Prewett line until closure.*

Top right - *As dirty as it had once been presentable. Last days at Basingstoke MPD.*

Right - *The former Alton line bay lasted in use well into BR days, used mainly for parcels traffic. The numbering '1A' will be noted. After the introduction of MAS signalling a colour light signal guarded the exit from the bay on to the main line, this particular signal surviving for some time after the actual trackwork in the bay platform was lifted: all the time displaying its red 'stop' indication. In 2001 a blue plaque, commemorating the former Light Railway to Alton was placed at the station.*

Top - A through Portsmouth to Reading service at Basingstoke in July 1957. These services were given over to DEMU operation from June 1958. Arthur Tayler - KR collection

Left - Following closure of the GWR station, a single platform remained in use with a run-round loop using the track of the other platform. This set of rails then continued around the rear of Platform 4 giving direct access to the loco sidings. (See plan on pages 30/31 of Issue 5.)

Top - Worting Junction looking west. The flyover seen in the lower view, referred to as Battledown Flyover, was off the up Bournemouth line, seen coming in on the right. The two centre sets of rails form the up and down West of England main lines. High speed crossovers are laid between the various routes. Curiously the signal box at Worting was of the conventional mechanical type.

Above - No. 31801 having climbed the 1 in 412 to the flyover is about to cross the West of England lines. The train will then descend at 1 in 106 via the right hand line seen in the top view. The bridge structure, (No 143A), was strengthened in June 1930 at a cost of £557 2s 6d, possibly to accommodate heavier locomotives.   John Davenport / The Transport Treasury

We would obviously have liked to include some views of the interior of the LSWR signal boxes at Basingstoke although for the present no exterior or interior views have been located - any offers for the future?

Instead here are three views of the low-pressure pneumatic signalling installation at Brookwood albeit in fairly late BR days. The box contained a frame of 40 levers consisting of 18 signals, 15 points, 2 control, and 5 spare levers. In later years Pirbright Junction signal box had been closed and control was then exercised from Brookwood: as witness the inclusion of the junction on the diagram. The levers of the frame stood at three-inch centres.

Classified by the Signalling Record Society as a 'Type 4' box, this was the standard style of signal box used in connection with the pneumatic installation between here and Basingstoke: slightly unusual though compared with most of the other structures along this stretch of line was the provision of a porch and external staircase. The box seen here was brought into use in July 1907. Prior to 1904 two signal boxes had controlled the layout.

The mechanical locking to the frame was housed in the cabinets beneath the levers. The lack of block-instruments indicates that track-circuit block with an illuminated diagram was in place on the main lines although 3-position block working was in place from Ash Vale. Although lit by electricity, an emergency oil-lamp hung from the ceiling, the base of which is just visible in the top right hand view. This was in place until the box closed from 5th June 1966.

All John Davenport / The Transport Treasury

WHAT THE WELL DRESSED SOUTHERN MAN WAS WEARING IN 1948...

The things that turn up at the bottom of boxes are sometimes remarkable. We present here one such case, with a selection of views taken around June 1948 outside what were the clothing stores at Lewisham. One un-named individual has been given the task of modelling a variety of serge attire: either that or he was multi-skilled or a member of a family of look-alikes!

Seriously though, as a break from trains, operation, rolling stock and some of the more obvious subjects, it is a welcome change to present a portrait of the normal working man. Unfortunately we have no idea who this man was, no name being recorded, instead at the time it was what he was showing that was more important. It was a style that had changed little in the past decades and indeed would continue unaltered until the major transitions that occurred in the sixties. (Didn't BR consult the fashion designer Hardy Amies in 1963 for a new range of work clothes? It was reported then that staff were seen displaying the then replacement 'new-look' uniforms at Waterloo in February 1964, the intention being to gauge reaction from both the staff themselves as well as

what were correctly identified as passengers.)

But returning to the present sequence of views: whilst the insignia on the various cap-badges is self explanatory, look more closely and there are often subtle changes that exist relative to the clothing style. Some of the grades would also soon disappear: did we still have 'Pointsman' in 1948? For that matter is the 'SR' referring to 'Southern Region' or 'Southern Railway'? The colour of the tunics was not reported.

What would nowadays be deemed 'multi-functionality' also applied even in 1948. An example being that seen opposite, where the uniform modelled was reported as applicable to, 'Bill Poster, Caller Off, Capstan Man, Carter, Checker - Senior, Cloak Room Attendant, Craneman, Crossing Keeper, Letter Sorter, Loader, Lost Property Attendant, Number Taker, Office-man, Office Lad, Repairer, Roper, Sheeter, Signal Lad, Signal Lampman and Lad, Stableman, Station Messenger, Telephone Attendant., Tracer, Van Lad, Van Setter, and Weighbridge-Man'. As they say, 'Vive le différence'.

For shunting at the south end of the Carriage Shop, latterly the transfer of vehicles from No 15 Road to either 13 or 14 Roads, the SR acquired a Thorneycroft petrol engined vehicle, possibly around 1934/35 and as a replacement for the Ford. The outside mirror and light will be noted although from the photographs, the former would appear to have just been on the one side. Given the number 499, later DS 499, it originally carried a a curved plate above the radiator proclaiming 'Southern Rly'. The sliding shutters to the cab will also be noted. From appearances at least, it is likely the vehicle was made around various SR components.

Tim Stubbs and F Foote

LANCING Part 2

The Southern Railway 1930 - 1947

(Continued from 'Southern Way No 6')

Eight Works Managers had charge of Lancing between 1912 and 1965: they were:

A H Panter 1912 – 1923 ("With the retirement due to ill health of Mr D Earle Marsh, the Locomotive, Carriage and Wagon Engineer, the Directors [of the LBSCR] decided that his assistants should take charge of their respective sections until the 31/12/1911. Accordingly, Mr. Panter became Carriage and Wagon Superintendent and took charge of the Carriage and Wagon Works at Lancing." W Panter, father of A N Panter, occupied a similar position as Rolling Stock Superintendent on the LSWR.)

G H Gardner 1923 – 1941 (In some records spelt as Gardener.)

O C Hackett 1941 – 1942

F B Illston 1942 – 1951

Charles E Collins 1951 – 1961 (Nicknamed 'Slasher' as he stopped all overtime as soon as he arrived.)

Leslie Cheeseman 1961 (For a short period only of between six to nine months.)

W (Dick) Levett 1961 – 1964

J Hiller 1964 - ?

George Clifford (Given the title 'Works Superintendent', reporting to the Works Manager at Eastleigh during the lead up to closure of the Works in 1965.)

The reorganisation of the Works, described in the previous instalment (see Southern Way No. 6), was partly attributable to the then Works Manager, Mr Gardner[1]. In 1927 he had suggested a number of changes to the existing working procedures, facilities and equipment, all with the aim of improving efficiency. Amongst these were to reduce the size of the Sawmill and use part of the resultant free space for the conversion of rolling stock. To this end items of machinery had to be repositioned including a 20-ton overhead crane. Consequential strengthening of the shop floor and associated electrical work was necessary, whilst outside, various sidings were altered. The total cost of these changes was recorded at £4,000.

Elsewhere he suggested the provision of a conveyor in the Carriage Shop to transport material stripped from coaches in the repair bays. For an outlay of £400 there would be an estimated saving of £150 per annum, presumably gauged on manpower / hour savings. Outside the shops a turntable was installed at the south end of the workshop which, "…would reduce the overtime by shunting staff", the latter no doubt unpopular with the men involved. This cost £200. Although not confirmed, it is likely this turntable was second-hand.

Ted Knight describes life at Lancing from the time he started as an Office Boy / Messenger in 1936 prior to his apprenticeship; "My first day in the employ

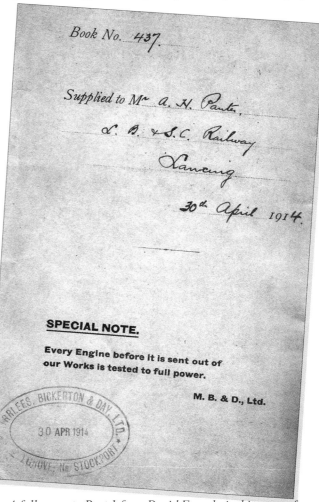

A follow up to Part 1 from David French, is this copy of the cover from the instruction book for the Mirrlees diesel-engines issued to Mr Panter in 1914.

ARP facilities at Lancing. Two such towers were provided within the works and two others outside. Their height was dictated in order to obtain the requisite angle of fire against low-flying enemy aircraft.

of the Southern Railway is stamped indelibly upon my mind. As a lad fresh from the sheltered life of the classroom now suddenly finding myself working in a giant railway works I felt that I had been flung in the deep end. No toe in first to test the water for me.

To attempt to describe the atmosphere within a railway works is very difficult, to say the least. It is a world all of its own, completely detached from the outside: a smelly, noisy, dusty, grimy world and to me at that tender age, a very frightening one. For ages it seemed that I hated that works and the drab Dickensian office. I had to summon up all my courage to continue my railway service and not let my father down. I was in fact afraid of being afraid and for just 9/6d per week.

Gradually though I warmed to the carriage shop office and with the help of, and no doubt the patience of, the office staff, I settled and mastered the duties expected of a messenger lad. I found my way around the works, I even learned to make the office tea.

The staff of the carriage shop office was

headed by Mr. Sands, Alf to many, but not to the two office boys, Jimmy Leggat and myself. Mr. Sands was a kindly man but a strict disciplinarian, at least where office boys were concerned. He was ably assisted by two clerks, Mr. Forward and Mr. Fuller and a junior clerk, Mr. Jackson.

Some of the clerical staff considered themselves rather aloof from all others, especially the manual workers, although in my experience as a messenger lad, I found nothing but kindness and consideration from the staff of the carriage shop office. The best way to get to know a factory or works is, I am sure, to become a messenger lad, as my duties took me everywhere. I also acted as a waiter in the Foreman's Mess, a position regarded as a perk. This was a coveted position landed for me through the kind offices of Mr. Sands, my boss. Mr. Sands, it seems, was never backward in pulling a few strings for what he considered a worthy cause.

As waiter or steward as the actual diners

A 'visitation' by the enemy, noon on 30th September 1942. Seen is the Panel Shop, with the camouflaged roof of the Cell Shop in the foreground. An amount of rolling stock was also damaged on either side of the building in this raid. Above the roof in the top view, can be seen the spotters tower referred to in the text.

This was one of at least four occasions enemy bombs hit rolling-stock stored in sidings around the works, although damage to the works themselves was minimal. It is believed any casualties were slight.

According to notes compiled by Dick Coombes and made available by John Atkinson, Lancing was attacked on two occasions. Firstly, on 25th April 1941 at 7.25 am, the area was hit by a high-explosive bomb resulting in one vehicle being written off and two other badly damaged. The identity of one of vehicles involved, 1305, is given. Then on 30th September 1942 enemy bombs again fell. This time two vehicles were badly damaged and 16 suffered what was considered to be slight damage. The numbers referred to are: 1256, 1485, 1507, 1776, 1883, 1847 and 3004.

Damaged Maunsell stock consequent upon the raid at 12.15 pm, 30th September 1942. It was unfortunate that some of stock damaged on this occasion was in fact freshly overhauled and had been ready to return to traffic. In the background it is just possible to discern a former LMS loco tender. Contemporary reports refer to there being several of these at the works for use as mobile water reservoirs and to assist the Works Fire-Brigade the men for which came from a variety of trades. Pre-war the brigade had worn polished brass helmets but these gave way to services style steel helmets soon after September 1939.

preferred to call me, I was required to work my dinner hour waiting at table, then take a late meal break. In return I would earn my dinner, a very good dinner, in fact the very same as I had been serving. Carrying out these duties I got to know many of the foremen and members of the managerial staff. I even knew their gastronomic likes and dislikes.

Every Friday an extra duty befell me, as this was pay-day for the works staff and the Works Manager, Mr. Gardner remained in his office during the midday break: I suppose this was due to the responsibility of the large amount of money on the premises. However he required that his own midday meal be served to him downstairs in his large office.

Mr. Gardener, every inch a manager, literally ruled Lancing Works: nobody challenged his authority, so for the young steward this was a daunting weekly ordeal. Before entering the office it was obligatory for

all to knock and await permission to enter; all well and good, but when bearing a large, well-laden, tray, this feat was not easy: whilst opening the door was made even more difficult by a rather powerful door closer. Upon gaining entry the main problem was yet to come, as Mr. Gardner didn't like his door closed noisily, so it was now necessary to deftly catch the rapidly closing door with the right foot and then gently allow it to close.

The meal delivered, I always beat a hasty retreat, happy to be out of that office. But later came another visit, this time with a cup of tea and to collect the tray and plates.

Through all this drama the Works Manager just sat at his desk watching, offering no help whatsoever, waiting it seemed to reprimand should the door bang. The sequel to this story is that on the last day before Christmas, Mr. Gardner slipped me a folded banknote, commenting, "That is for the entertainment you have

OVS Bulleid, (standing right) and Sir Eustace Missenden (standing centre), watching staff at work in making tail plane units for Horsa gliders in the Pullman Car Shop.

The office staff at Lancing had their own separate system of booking-in. Some recall the clerical department personnel as always seemingly dressed in sombre attire.

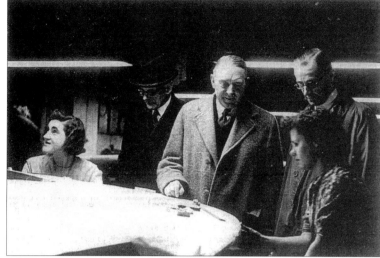

Workers from the bombed Panel Shed where Pontoons were made. A look-out tower is visible in the background. Under the standard working conditions as applied in industry, accidents were fairly commonplace although most minor injuries could be dealt with by the permanent first-aid man within the special medical room. More serious cases were taken to hospital by taxi or a summoned ambulance. Whilst the works had its own well- equipped Fire Brigade, no similar ambulance vehicle was ever provided.

given me throughout the year!" Outside the manager's office I found that I was 10/- richer. I think it is true to say that no doors were closed to the messenger-cum-steward. I worked in the carriage shop office for thirteen and a half months, up until my sixteenth birthday. Prior to this time I had to choose the trade I wished to follow. To be perfectly honest I wasn't keen on following any trade, I was happy where I was, but this was not possible. I had to choose a trade or leave. Why I had found this office so dull and depressing in those first few weeks I could not now understand: I was now loath to leave both it and the friendliness of the staff.

After due consideration and with the help from the foremen I chose the trade of a coach finisher. So I reluctantly bade farewell to both office and the foreman's mess-room, and those very nice meals, from now on it would be sandwiches for me."

Within the works, the 1930s saw a continuation of work under the 'Progressive' scheme described previously, a situation which was sustained until the outbreak of war in September 1939. For unknown reasons, many of the trades at Lancing were not on the 'reserved occupations list' and consequently men were served with call-up papers to be replaced in their roles by women. As the conflict continued, so women could be found as welders, operating capstan latches and on other machine work. Additionally, they were employed as pipe fitters mate as well as what might have been expected to be a more female type of occupation, trimming and sewing-machine work.

To deal with the administrative requirements of the female workforce, two former SECR Pullman cars, 'Albatross' and 'Thistle' were brought into the yard and stabled near to the power house.[2] They served as office accommodation for Miss Hawkes, the manager of the female staff. The Works Manager would also avail himself of the sleeping accommodation they provided if he was required to remain on-site at night. Subsequent to 1945 the two vehicles were used as offices for the Progressive Repair Scheme.

The proximity of the works to the coast, a matter of yards from the coast road (A259), meant it was in the front line relative to attack from enemy aircraft

Left - *Coach Finishers, photographed in 1943. Back row, L-R: Jim Edwards, Fred Long, Bill Shute. Front row, L-R: Frank Goodall, Frank Ashdown.*

Bottom - *Reproduced from the Nov/ Dec 1942 issue of 'The Southern Railway Magazine', with apologies for the poor quality. The view depicts a, "... load of over 40 four-wheeled 'cov-cars' leaving an SR Works [obviously Lancing] behind No C3." The tare weight of the train was reported as 520 tons.*

arriving low across the channel. Bitter experience dictated that the Luftwaffe could arrive before the local air-raid siren was activated, this from information received from the RAF and Royal Observer Corps. In an attempt to counter this danger and so give some opportunity for the workforce to take cover, a 'spotters' tower' was constructed on the roof of the Pullman Car shop, manned by works personnel who had been trained to identify differing aircraft types. The men here worked a 'four hours on / fours hour off' routine. Should the enemy be sighted, then an alarm was activated which rang in every shop. The workforce would then take cover in the various workshop pits, at the bottom of which had been placed old carriage cushions, whilst at intervals above the pits were rolled steel joists. There were also several specially constructed outside air-raid shelters sunk into the ground. Messrs Blackford and Ames in their history of Lancing, report the drivers of the 20-ton overhead travelling cranes were the least envied under these conditions, for the sounding of the alarm bells coincided with an immediate shut down of the electricity supply, consequently the crane may well

have halted in any position. The crane driver had then to descend by rope ladder thrown out of the cab. The outside shelters were where the football ground was later located and could hold 100 workers including an ARP warden and ambulance man. The procedure was that as each person entered he would hand the warden a ticket with his name. This was then put in a circular metal container which, when full, was thrown out of the shelter by the warden. the idea being that if the shelter were to take a direct hit, there would be some record as to who had been present.

Initially the workforce were making their way to the shelters every time a warning was sounded, but this naturally resulted in much disruption to work. Consequently it was left to the 'spotters' on the roof, who would only ring the warning bell when an aircraft was actually sighted, and the workforce was instructed not to take cover until the final bell was heard. Despite what might then appear to be an increased risk to their personal safety, these changes were accepted by the workforce. Indeed according to an article by John Walker as appears on the internet[3], "For the 54 years

Viewed inside the works from the height of the overhead travelling crane. These cranes were of 20 ton capacity. In the event of an air-raid warning sounding whilst working the fastest way for the crane driver to reach the ground and seek the safety of shelter was by means a rope ladder.

Tim Stubbs

that the Works were open there was no form of industrial dispute and the workers were extremely loyal."

To protect the works from enemy air attack, two separate 'Bofors' anti-aircraft guns were located within the works perimeter. However in order to obtain the requisite angle of fire against a low flying enemy, these guns were of necessity mounted on towers 20-30 feet high. As such the members of the Works Home Guard responsible for the guns were distinctly vulnerable. As a means of affording some degree of escape from a machine-gunning aircraft, a five feet depth of coal dust was spread around the base of the towers. This was intended to form some sort of soft landing place should the gunners have to jump to safety. Two more guns, this time outside the works, in the vicinity of Western Road, were manned by army personnel. At the south end of the Paint Shop a small office was converted for use of a regular Army armourer, who would service and maintain all four gun emplacements. One aerial attack resulted in a bomb hitting the Panel Shop close to the Pullman Shop. The blast from this blew away the access ladders to the spotters tower. The men were not harmed, although they

remained marooned for some time until a temporary ladder could be rigged to reach them. A replacement spotters' tower, some 30 feet high, was then erected between the main approach sidings to the yard. Whilst aerial attacks caused disruption and damage to the works, it is not believed there were any fatalities on site. Outside the works though, one of the guns on the perimeter was the subject of a direct bomb hit, killing all the Army personnel.

Additional to the normal scheduled repair work undertaken, was the forced additional work caused by repairs to damaged rolling stock plus, in common with the other Southern workshops, specific war work. This included pontoon boats for the Army and the tail sections of 'Horsa' gliders. This war work was conducted in the Pullman shop and three roads of the Paint Shop, entry to both being restricted. In consequence these areas of manufacture were referred to as the 'Hush-Hush' shop.

Within the Smiths' Shop were made 'drop stamp' parts for 25-pound guns, plus other, unspecified, naval items. Prior to 1944, three complete ambulance trains were built (it may have been that this was just a fitting-out exercise) for use of the American Forces and

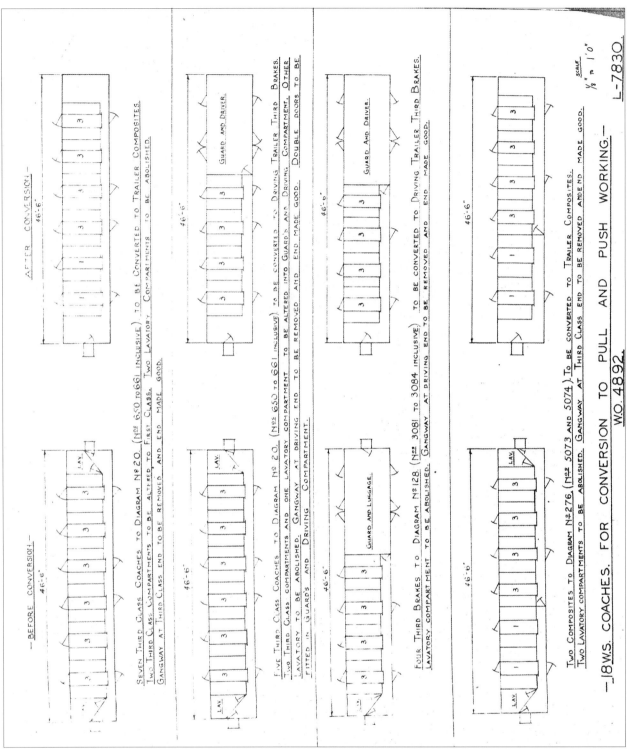

Amongst the work carried out at Lancing during the war years, were these 1943 Pull-Push conversions from former LSWR stock. A few years earlier in peace-time, one of the prestige pre-war tasks had been fitting out of coaching stock for the new 'Bournemouth Limited', the interior of which was finished in the then fashionable 'Rexine' cloth, also referred to as 'American Cloth' – a form of pseudo / imitation leather.

Courtesy David Wigley

which were later used in France. In effect these were a complete mobile hospital, comprising boiler car – for steam and electricity generation, pharmacy, operating, sleeping, catering and ward cars.

Morale was of course an important facet of the time in ensuring productivity and included more than one occasion when an edition of the BBC 'Workers Playtime' was broadcast live from Lancing, the announcer telling the listeners it was coming to them from, 'Somewhere in England'. Part of this morale boosting also came in the form of the first official mid-morning break, official records stating that on 30th February 1942 an order was placed for new canteen facilities at the works, to be located in a separate building south of the Paint Shop. These were substantial facilities as the estimated cost was £16,750. Around the same time there was also a long overdue improvement in sanitary facilities.

Post-1939, there were also improvements to clocking-in, although still using the 'pay-check' procedure. There were changes to the previous pay-day procedure, meaning the workers were no longer required to form long queues in the open air outside the pay office and could instead wait in the comparative comfort of the inside of the shops. This change was brought about owing to fear of casualties should a low-flying enemy aircraft suddenly appear.

Notwithstanding this, war or no war, there was no relaxation in the strict procedures governing booking-on, again as recounted by Ted Knight."Time, always of paramount importance to the Southern, meant that little leeway was given to any worker failing to keep good time. To ensure that the workmen had no plausible excuse for bad time keeping, the age-old method to remind all of the hour, a system of hooters was employed. Before the final starting hooter sounded, a three minute warning was given by three short blasts, this gave anyone within striking distance sufficient time to arrive at the time office and pick up their check, thus 'booking on'. There was, I might add, some-thing of a stampede to reach the time office before the final hooter ceased and the windows closed down, failure to do so resulted in the loss of a quarter of an hour's pay. Consistent unpunctuality could and did mean the loss of employment." What arrangements and allowance existed in the event of the 'Lancing Belle' running late or in the event of the need to seek shelter from enemy aircraft was not reported.

With a return to peace, a social revolution swept through Lancing, in the same way as it affected every other workplace in industry. A Works Committee now dealt with welfare issues and with a Socialist Government in power and Nationalisation on the horizon, hopes for the future were high.

The workload also remained consistent, catching up with arrears of maintenance which had occurred during the war years, whilst in addition there was much to do to restore the Pullman fleet to the requisite standard. To assist in this latter task, skilled trimmers were seconded from Lancing to the Pullman works at Preston Park.

As before, the compilation of this article would not have been possible without reference to 'Railway Recollections. A Memento of Lancing Carriage and Wagon Works' by John H Blackford and Jerry Ames. Further information has come from the memoirs of the late Ted Knight or as stated in the text, captions and footnotes.

The final instalment on the subject of Lancing, will deal with the BR period and the lead up to the closure of the Works.

(1) Ted Knight, who commenced at Lancing in 1936, comments on the hierarchy of the Works thus: "To organize any large concern efficiently there must be a managerial staff, and Lancing Works was no exception for it had a manager, two under-managers, its shop foremen and under-foremen and on the shop floor its chargemen. For The Southern Railway this was sufficient to run the works; but with the advent of British Railways everyone, it seemed, had to have an assistant!" (The workforce was stated to have been around 1,800 in the immediate post-war period decreasing then in the years leading up to closure. It may be reasonable to assume the figure was slightly less than this in pre-war days, with the peak levels being achieved during WW2. It is not thought Lancing ever worked a permanent 3-shift system, although during wartime some men would continue late into the evening to complete urgent work. With delays attributable to air-raid warnings, sometimes the finishing time was not until 3.00 am.)

(2) In 1896 The Metropolitan Carriage and Wagon Company, Birmingham, built eight vehicles to the order of the S.E.R. They were built to the limit of the Hastings branch loading gauge, the body length being 50 ft. and the width over the body sills being 8 ft. 5½ in. (i.e., the limit for that length of body). The cars were withdrawn shortly after the outbreak of the First World War (probably on 6th August 1914), and were rebuilt by the Pullman Car Company in 1918/19 to become Pullman cars. *Thistle* and *Albatross*, as they became known, were originally brake-thirds before their transformation to Pullmans. They required remodelling completely. Internally, the rebuilding of these cars was such as to bring them as far as possible to Pullman standards, including lavish marquetry, table lamps, armchairs, etc. The original multi-light doors were retained and the cars

LANCING BR
Courtesy David Wigley

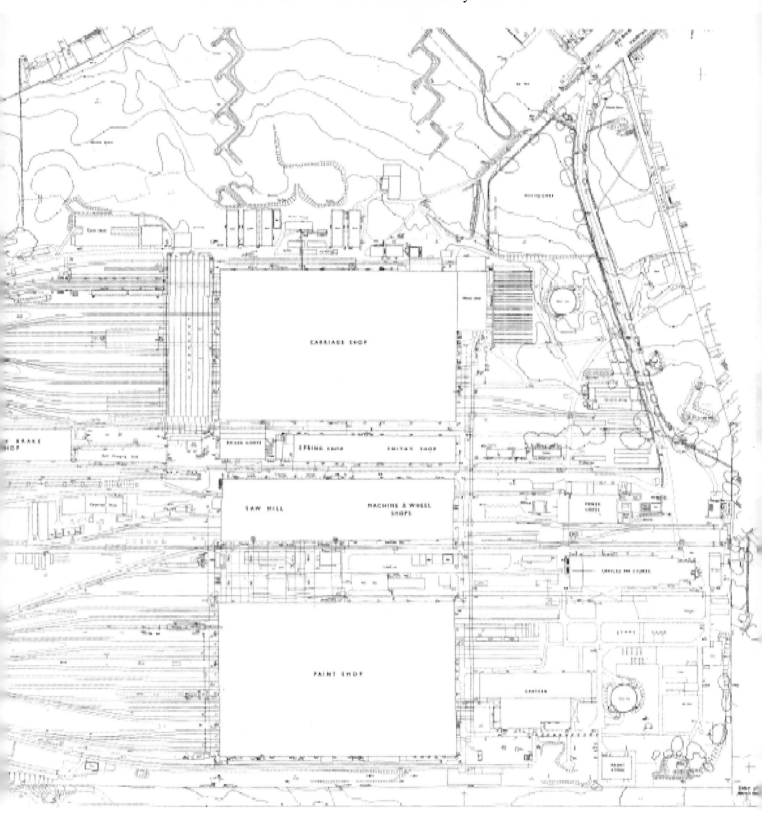

were finished in the Pullman red livery, and were classed as 'type D'. All eight cars were withdrawn from traffic by 1930, still finished in the Pullman red livery, but *Thistle* and *Albatross* had a further lease of life by undergoing a second rebuilding by the Pullman Company. This time they became 'supply' cars – in effect kitchen cars – and had no passenger accommodation at all. The alterations were confined to the interiors, and the only change in external appearance was that most of the windows were glazed with artic glass. These two cars, as rebuilt, entered traffic in 1931 finished in Pullman umber all over; otherwise their appearance (except for the mottled windows) was

similar to other Pullman cars and the names allocated in 1918/19 were retained. The word 'Pullman' along the fascia boards was, however, dropped, and was replaced by a third centrally-placed scroll. These two supply cars were finally withdrawn from traffic in 1938, but were subsequently sent to Lancing where they served as additional office accommodation. Several of their sisters, the erstwhile *Hilda* and *Dorothy* at least, survive to this day as privately-owned grounded bungalows located on the South Coast. *Thistle* and *Albatross* remained at Lancing, in their same physical position, until 1964 when they were repositioned by the steam works shunter on the breaking up-sidings and

dismantled. (The breaking-up sidings were a pair of sidings south of the main line and on the west side of the shunters' box.) – with grateful thanks to Antony Ford based on notes from J Howard Turner.

(3)Ref:http://www.northlancing.com/History/The%20history%20of%20Lancing%20Railway%20Carriage%20Works/Lancing%20Railway%20Carriage%20works%20history.htm

(The story of the Southern in Wartime is recounted in 'Southern Way Special No 3 – Wartime Southern', currently available. 'Wartime Southern Part 2' is also in preparation. See inside cover for more information.)

Opposite page - The 'Lancing Belle' with its numbered compartments awaiting departure during the BR era. The numbered compartments will be noted. (For an explanation of this see the previous instalment). En-route, and in a gesture hardly considered friendly by the recipient, workers travelling on the 'Lancing Belle' would throw rivets on to the allotment of a fellow riveter from the Works whose land was located alongside the railway. Tim Stubbs

Above - A Southern Region era view inside the works and showing vehicles at various stages of repair. Tim Stubbs

Left - Examples of two of the three types of pay-check used. The missing one was circular.

Bottom - Redundant vehicles literally out to grass alongside the works. It is believed they were once used as storage.

SPOTLIGHT DORCHESTER

For a period during the 1950s, the monthly 'Southern Region Magazine', as successor to the 'Southern Railway Magazine', printed a regular 'Spotlight' feature on its rear cover featuring a particular station or location. Whilst we have access to several of these issues, in bound form the covers were invariably removed and hence we have no idea if the station at Dorchester South ever featured. As a tribute though to what may now be considered to be a most useful regular piece to the modeller and historian, we present what will be the first in an occasional series of station 'Spotlights'. (The next to feature is likely to be Crawley.)

Dorchester South was unusual so far as the Southern was concerned, I hesitate to say unique as someone will no doubt contradict me, but unusual in so far as trains in the up direction scheduled to stop, had of necessity to pull forward and then set back into the up platform which was itself a dead end. The same did not apply for down trains, as from 5th May 1879 a platform was provided for down trains on the curve leading to the line to Weymouth.

The reason for this strange arrangement has been told oft times previously so will only be précised here. Suffice to say the original Southampton and Dorchester Railway, more often referred to in part at least as the 'Castleman's Corkscrew', (so named after the original promoter Charles Castleman and the tortuous route taken particular west of Brockenhurst as far as Hamworthy), was intended to be part of a route from Southampton to Exeter. Had this come about, Dorchester would have been a through station on the line westwards.

For reasons that were both financial and geographical, it was the route west from Salisbury that was eventually favoured and what had then intended to be a through station at Dorchester ended up as terminus.

This arrangement lasted from the time of opening, on 1st June 1847, for just under ten years, that is until 20th January 1857 at which time a south-facing curve was provided to connect with the GWR Wilts Somerset & Weymouth line and so afford access to Weymouth. Even so, it was not until more than 20 years later, and as referred to previously, that a platform was provided on this curve. Nothing further ever came of a west facing extension for the LSWR or its successors, and up trains from Weymouth continued to reverse into the platform at what was later known as Dorchester South. This arrangement continued until as late as June 1970 and outlasted steam traction, even if the sight of a push-pull fitted Class 33 and accompanying TC set did somehow look distinctly out of place performing such a manoeuvre on a supposedly swish modern railway.

The alternative to the reversing of trains was the obvious provision of a second platform for up workings on the south curve. One may wonder why such a facility was not provided earlier and the original station given over to parcels and terminating services? But evidently this was not an urgent consideration for the LSWR or SR as although the original timber overall roof was removed around 1938, a modern canopy in the then standard SR style was provided on the terminal platform probably at the same time.

Goods facilities were extensive and previously have rarely been seen, indeed views of goods yards generally are often rare, but we are glad to report the goods shed at Dorchester and station forecourt can now be seen in some detail.

The station even had its own locomotive shed, again a throwback to the days of the terminus and which survived far longer than perhaps might have been expected, officially closing on 17th June 1957.

Opposite page - The up platform at Dorchester South probably recorded circa 1960 and seen from the down platform: located on the curve to the Weymouth line. The modern and airy appearance of the canopy, provided circa 1938, is apparent. An overall roof had originally been provided at the western end of this platform, together with a short island platform facing both the terminus run round loop and up line from Weymouth. Surprisingly this was little used and was removed around the same time. Access between the up and down platforms was via a subway, the roof of which is visible just by the platform ramp. *Right* - Trespass notice facing the site of the former engine shed. South Western Cottages on Cromwell Road and Alfred Road are in the background.

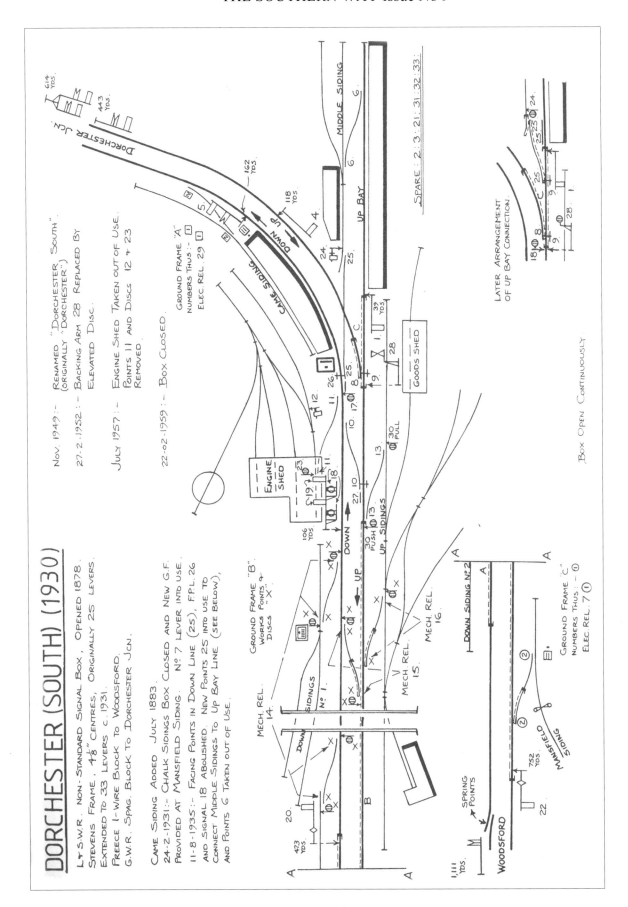

Left - *The signal box at Dorchester was unusual in that the frame was positioned at 90° to the running lines. Opened in 1878 it was of the elevated type and contained a frame of 25 levers, later extended to 33 levers. The original LSWR box was superseded in 1959 by a modern BR structure situated close to where the down sidings join the main line. George Pryer*

This page - *Dorchester South engine shed, showing the original 1847 two-road brick structure and later, 1857, two-road extension. Only a small turntable, 50' diameter, was provided and whilst this was sufficient in early years, it was s severe handicap later. According to Hawkins and Reeve in 'Southern Sheds' (OPC), there had been plans to transfer the 65' turntable from Exmouth Junction to Dorchester, but this never took place and no turntable was ever provided. Seen are the interior of the original shed and archways connecting to the later extension, also what was one of the artisans' workshops. S C Townroe was Shed-Master at Dorchester, it is believed, prior to WW2. Under BR, the depot was given the designation 71C and had an allocation of locomotives of the 'T9', 'G6', 'O2', 'L12', 'U' and 'E4' types. A little surprisingly two 'Lord Nelson' locos, 30864 and 30865 were also shown as allocated here between April and October 1954. The most modern type was a pair of BR Class 4 4-6-0s, 76005 and 76006 from April 1954 to February 1955. All S C Townroe / R Blencowe collection Further information on Dorchester South may be found in 'Southern stations' by Pryer and Bowring, and more recently in the two volume Oakwood set, Castleman's Corkscrew' by Brian Jackson.*

This page - Top and centre, the down platform viewed from the up platform with an attempt at least, of some form of garden in what at this point at least, was otherwise waste land in-between the two. Where the 'V' between the two diverging lines widened further was for many years the headquarters of the Dorset Constabulary.

Bottom view - Looking across to the up platform. Until 1879 both up and down trains had used the one platform, each having to perform a reverse manoeuvre if heading towards or arriving from Weymouth and calling at Dorchester en-route.

Opposite page - The exterior of the up platform, dated of course by the design of cars on view. Whether by accident or design, the colonnades give an impression of importance, indeed as befits a station for what was the county town of Dorsetshire. Whether the brick infills were original or supplemented an earlier pattern structure is not reported. An overall roof had once existed above the public entrance.
This and pages 68/69 - Paul Hersey collection

Pages 68/69 overleaf - The goods yard and goods shed seen from within the yard and also looking across from the down platform. By this stage, coal would appear to be the principal commodity handled, a number of staiths and coal bins on the opposite side of the siding to where the line of mineral wagons are positioned. Left of the goods shed in the main view, were three sidings one of which fronted a set of cattle pens, Dorchester having for many years a thriving livestock market. There was also a short private siding off the goods yard for the local brewer, Messrs Eldridge Pope and Co. whose Dorchester Brewery was immediately north of the goods yard. The original goods shed dated from 1847 but was extended twice, first in 1884 and then again in 1897.
Paul Hersey collection

This page - *Stages in the shunting of a passenger train from Weymouth into the Up Platform. In the view top left, the up train, behind No. 34087 '145 Squadron' arrives from Weymouth and is then seen (top right) coming to a halt ahead of the backing signal. (This signal was originally of the standard LSWR horizontal 'X' type, as per the well-known example at Evercreech Junction, but was replaced later, probably around 1959, by an elevated disc on the same post. The position of this signal can be seen in the top view on the opposite page.) With the backing signal then cleared, No 28 on the signal diagram, the train was then clear to set-back into the platform: naturally under the guiding arm of the Guard and station staff. In the lower left view, the train is seen awaiting departure with No 1 signal, in the 'off' position. Finally in the lower right view, the train is seen getting away. The average length of time for this manoeuvre including the station stop at Dorchester was only in the order of two to three minutes. The buffer stops at the end siding form the conclusion of the single line through the goods shed.*

Opposite top - *Vans parked in the up siding alongside the goods shed, the two running lines presently clear of traffic. The view is looking east towards Moreton and eventually Bournemouth. Notice the backing signal referred to has been superseded by an elevated disc. The loco shed has also been demolished and the sidings removed. The buffer stop on the right is at the end what was referred to as Came siding, accessed from a trailing connection at the south end of the down platform and controlled from a separate electrically released, ground-frame. Post 1970, this siding was extended back to the new signal box with a new trailing connection from the down line. The railway cottages seen on the right have been mentioned previously, whilst a further eight dwellings for railway staff were located on the opposite side of the line. The area of waste ground had once formed sidings for the loco depot, engine access to which was not ideal as it involved a shunt move into the first of the shed roads before reversing back if access were required to any of the other roads. With the shed and sidings removed the area, for a while at least, became a coal dumping ground.*

Opposite bottom - *No. 30743 'Lyonnesse' waiting at the up platform on 20th September 1952. The Southern Railway were evidently not in any hurry to remove the supports to the side of the former train shed, preferring to leave BR to deal with this! The subway between the platforms, officially bridge No 121 and referred to earlier, is also identified.*

Paul Hersey collection (5) and A E West (1).

'DELTICS' FOR THE SOUTHERN REGION?

Paul Heathcote

The 'Deltic' diesel class, introduced on the Eastern Region of British Railways in 1961/62, was a revolution so far as modernising the services on the east-coast main line was concerned. Conceived as a replacement for the various Gresley and Peppercorn Pacific types, its rated power output of 3,300 horse-power meant it was possible to accelerate trains to speeds hitherto unheard of, and proved yet again that the advantage of modern traction was not just in terms of acceleration but in being able to maintain higher speeds uphill. To be fair, such improvements had also only become possible because of improvements to the permanent way, allowing for sustained high speed running – your author vividly recalls a contemporary article in which it was stated the 22 'Deltic' locos would replace no less than 55 steam engines, such was their conceived availability, whilst their performance on gradients like the famed climb to Stoke summit was such as to beat anything that could have been achieved with an A1, A3 or A4 Pacific. (The fact the A2 was omitted implies that on a good day the predicted 'Deltic' performance might then have been equalled. But it must be recalled, the historic wondrous performance of steam we have come to admire was often the product of a one-off output by both men and machine and hardly equal to the predicted every-day output of a new 'Deltic'.)

So far as dieselisation was concerned, the Eastern Region was to be in the forefront of high-power diesel traction. The LMR, in its interim use of diesel types, was forced to concede that its modern motive power was in fact inferior to the Stanier Pacifics, whilst the unreliability of the early Warship diesels on the WR meant it was not until 1962 and the arrival of the 'Western' class that the WR had for itself a reliable and powerful motive power unit, albeit at a mere 2,700 hp output. Interestingly, most of these early big diesel types comprised twin power units, often adapted from earlier proven types, the stated advantage being that should one

engine fail then the complete locomotive, and therefore the train, was less likely to become a cripple. Offset against this was additional weight and engineering complexity.

The Southern Region of course was different. Not only had it only ventured into dieselisation in a relatively small way, its principal use of modern traction was in the form of electricity although it must also be remembered that as late as 1964 no firm decision had yet been taken as to the future modernisation of the Bournemouth line, this despite the fact that steam locos were being withdrawn in ever increasing numbers.

So where does this all fit in so far as the title of this article is concerned? Well, simply, following the appearance of the prototype 'Deltic' in 1955, such was impact it created that both the LMR and ER were more than keen to utilise this latest example of modern transport technology. As of course is known, the ER case was approved, that for the LMR rejected, on the basis that 'Deltic' would have been a simple interim along the route towards electrification out of Euston. For the LMR, 'Deltic' would have been a too expensive stop-gap, with little potential use on the LMR after their first stage overhead electrification, post 1966 – unless, that is, the SR might have even have seen the type as its own modernisation power for the Bournemouth line – post LMR? But that is not quite what is now up for debate, although it is certainly another possibility, just like the 1965/66 plan to transfer redundant Stanier Pacifics to the SR to replace unserviceable Bulleid Pacifics, although in that case it is likely they would have been seen running around with WD type tenders to ensure sufficient water supply [1]. (It has been suggested the transfer of LMR locos did not in the end take place due to clearance issues relative to Battledown flyover, perhaps a 'SW' reader can clarify the transfer issue.)

Instead we need to turn the clock back a few years to 4th July 1957 and a meeting of senior Southern

Opposite top - *'Lord Nelson' locos being made ready for Ocean Liner Workings at Eastleigh. Left, No. 30850 4th August 1952, and right, No. 30855: 7th February 1955, notice the oil cans, etc, on the buffer beam of 'Lord Nelson'. Most shipping lines seemed to have one of these wooden headboards, colourfully decorated and stored at Eastleigh against the inside wall of a grounded coach body - presumably there was a second headboard similarly stored at Nine Elms? The circular 'Cunarder' board was superseded by a rectangular shape in later years.*
Opposite bottom - *What might have been, well almost. BR No. 55002, the former D9002, 'Kings own Yorkshire Light Infantry' photographed on 19th November 1981 shortly before withdrawal. This locomotive subsequently became part of the National Collection. John Dedman*

One can almost imagine the harrassed shed foreman finding he had no choice but to turn out 'S15' No. 30511 for the down 'Greek Lines' boat train seen near Shawford on 2ⁿᵈ August 1958. Whilst such an occasion might well have cheered the photographer at the time as well as still being the subject of comment 50 years later, it was certainly not the image the operators wished to portray. A Deltic on such a working would have been very different, although of course faster progress could only have been made subject to line capacity. Interestingly the first vehicle is a former GWR 'Syphon'.

Tony Molyneaux / KR Collection

Region officers at which the topic of discussion was the possibility of the interim dieselisation of the Western Section of the SR, or a part of it at least. Specifically mentioned at the time was the likely timetable for electrification, viz 1967, a date that would indeed prove to be correct. This was followed by a full report on the topic, which is used as the basis for this article. This appeared on 1ˢᵗ August 1958.

The principal aim of the scheme appears to have been to meet the need to "…enhance the standing of the Ocean Liner trains to and from Southampton Docks as an interim measure pending electrification of the route in about 1967…". At the time the railway could hardly have seen themselves as under the threat from air competition. The crashes involving the Comet jet airliners had meant there was still no successful regular jet service although that would come very soon with the introduction in 1958 of the Boeing 707. From the above statement it might even be perceived that electrification was seen as the panacea for all potential

passenger complaints, although to be fair it must also be said that half a century later this is still the professed viewpoint.

The report continues with some interesting statistics. Taking the year 1957 as a whole, a total of 684 Ocean Liner trains were run from Waterloo to Southampton Docks, with 497 in the opposite direction. Of these 100 services in the down direction and 50 in the up direction were scheduled into the regular timetable. These were the 9.21 am and 10.35 am trains from Waterloo on Thursday each week, and the 9.43 am from Southampton on a Friday. They coincided with the regular sailings of Union-Castle line vessels. All other workings were run under Special Traffic arrangements, indicated in the regular Special Traffic Notices and in set 'Q' paths.

The number of additional workings also varied according to the month of the year. February saw the fewest, with 29 down and 19 up workings, whilst in the heaviest month, August, the figures were 100 and 55 respectively. Additionally, it was reported that one (unspecified) day in June 1957 witnessed 5 down and 10 up trains, and was the most on any one day of the year. Some days also saw trains only running in one direction only, or even no trains at all. The figures for these being 138 days on which no trains ran from Waterloo, 162 days when there was no service from Southampton Docks, and 70 days of the year in which there were no boat trains in either direction.

Understandably the whole scenario was a nightmare to the operators: finding sufficient locomotives, stock and crews when necessary, whilst on others days seeing valuable assets standing around not earning revenue.

At the time the management of the Southern Region and indeed BR itself, still viewed these special workings as being of some importance, as in 1958 they believed it desirable to have five new trains of, '… modern coaching stock each including a Pullman car and / or buffet car, together with two separate trains of just Pullman cars'. Together it was estimated, these would cover approximately 80 / 85% of the annual Ocean Liner traffic. Some additional spare stock would still be required when the occasion demanded.

It may well be that even the above statement is enough to generate a gasp from the reader. But more (better / worse – dependent upon the viewpoint) is about to come. For at the same time it was commented that the only suitable modern locomotive able to deal with

the weights and speeds required were the new 'Deltic' type diesel, although it was admitted this had yet to be proved in ordinary intensive service, the anticipated performance being based solely upon the remarkable success of the single prototype.

In some ways what followed now was almost reminiscent of Bulleid a decade earlier, when he had set his criteria for the intended performance and versatility of 'Leader'. Thus we read that a single unit diesel must be able to haul and heat trains of up to 450 tons trailing load and make full use of the permissible maximum track speed. At the time this was 60 mph in the suburban area and 85 mph elsewhere. The aim was for a 80 minute schedule ('or less') between Waterloo and Northam Junction with a full load. Ten years later, the 4-car 'REP' sets hauling an eight coach trailing load were regularly timed at 60 minutes between these two points when on the non-stop headcode '91' Waterloo – Southampton workings. This was of course subject to a clear run whilst the line speed had also been raised to an official 90 mph maximum (which was frequently being exceeded). This is mentioned as the power of a 4-REP set was 3,200 hp, only slightly less than the 3,300 hp of a 'Deltic'. Even so the weight of a 12-coach 4-REP/4-TCx2 combination at around 400 tons, was somewhat less than the proposed 450 ton trailing load and 105 ton locomotive. (The prototype 'Deltic' tipped the scales at 105 tons, the production models were slightly less at 99 tons.)

Another 4-6-0, although this time an unidentified member of the 'N15' class, No. 30478 perhaps? The location is just south of that referred to on the opposite page. The headboard proclaims 'The South American'. The stock is particularly interesting, including a former Pullman as the fifth vehicle in use here as a Restaurant Car. 2nd August 1958.

One obvious alterative already, or shortly to be, available, to the Region would have been the use of the BRCW Type 3 diesel-electric locomotives in the D65xx series then under construction. These though were already stated to lack sufficient power for such workings on their own, whilst multiple-unit operation would create difficulties at Waterloo due to the additional length of train involved.

Ever the pessimist, the SR considered a fleet of no less than seven 'Deltics' would be required to operate the trains, basing this criterion on ensuring four were simultaneously available for traffic. The high number of spare machines considered necessary as "...the traffic availability of a small batch of this particular type of locomotive could not be expected to be as favourable as with a larger fleet". It was almost as if the management were talking down the advantages of diesel, but perhaps with good reason. To date the only experience the region had had with large main line diesel locomotives had been with Nos 10201 – 3 and 10000 – 1. All had performed reasonably, albeit with a propensity to deposit oil in large quantities where it was least

desirable, but their reliability was not always ideal. In fairness this was only partly the fault of the designs. Lack of familiarity amongst operating and maintenance crews, as well as the attempt to service what were, for the time, high-tech machines within a steam shed environment, hardly created ideal conditions for reliability. The SR seems also to have forgotten the biggest disadvantage of all in the early diesel types, the unreliable steam-heating boiler, difficulties and failures with which accounted for a high proportion of the time the engines were out of service.

But they were learning fast so far as the needs for a different service environment was concerned. Consequently it was reported that the suggested seven locomotives could be serviced at the new diesel maintenance depot being provided at Stewarts Lane, although daily inspections, servicing and fuelling would still be carried out at Nine Elms. 'Garaging' and fuelling facilities would also be needed at Eastleigh. The Nine Elms option was of course far from adequate, whilst the existing facilities for diesel traction, as then provided at Eastleigh, were to be extended.

FRIDAY, 7th JUNE

No. 1—Special Stop

Time	From	To	Call specially	Purpose	Station to remit Trainmen
p.m. 9 0 ..	Waterloo ..	So'ton Old Docks ..	Winchester City ..	Set down passengers	Basingstoke

No. 2—Train Alterations, etc.

Train	From	To	Remarks	Service No.
			DOWN	
a.m. 6‖52 ..	Brockenhurst ..	Lymington Town ..	**Will not run.**	
7 40 .. (Parcels)	Clapham Jct. ..	Eastleigh and Southampton Docks	Revised	3
8 22 Q ..	Waterloo ..	So'ton Old Docks ..	**Will run. 'United States'. Train No. B.21**	—
8 54 Q ..	Waterloo ..	So'ton Old Docks ..	**Will run. 'United States'. Train No. B.22**	—
9‖ 0 ..	Brockenhurst ..	Bournemouth Ctl. ..	**Will not run.**	
9 20 ..	Birkenhead ..	Bournemouth West	**Revised from Southampton Central**	13
9 43 ..	Waterloo ..	So'ton Old Docks ..	Additional. 'United States'. Train No. B.23 ..	4
10 23 ..	York ..	Bournemouth West..	**Revised from Eastleigh**	21
10 45 ..	Winchester City ..	Southampton Term.	Depart Eastleigh 11.4 a.m. and run 2 minutes later thence.	—
11 50 ..	Sheffield ..	Bournemouth Ctl. ..	Relief to 10.23 a.m. ex York	18
11 55 ..	Wolverhampton ..	Bournemouth Ctl. ..	Additional. (Relief to 9.20 a.m. Birkenhead).. ..	9 &
p.m. 12 35 ..	Waterloo ..	Weymouth ..	**Additional Passenger**	5
12 35 Q ..	Waterloo ..	Southampton Docks	Pathway not available.	—
1 20 Q ..	Waterloo ..	Southampton Docks	Pathway not available.	—
1 22 ..	Waterloo ..	Bournemouth West..	**Additional Passenger**	
1 29 ..	Fareham ..	Bournemouth West..	**Revised from St. Denys**	
2 10 ..	Winchester City ..	Bournemouth Ctl. ..	**Revised from Brockenhurst**	1
2 30 ..	Waterloo ..	Weymouth ..	**Additional Passenger**	1
2 45 Q ..	Waterloo ..	Southampton Docks	Pathway not available.	
2 57 ..	Bournemouth Ctl. ..	Weymouth ..	**Start 3.2 p.m. and revised**	
3 14 ..	Waterloo ..	Bournemouth Ctl. ..	**Additional Passenger**	
3 20 ..	Waterloo ..	Weymouth and Bournemouth West	Revised	15 &

So far the proposal might perhaps have seemed reasonable, although what followed next in the report makes almost unbelievable reading. It starts with comment as to fact, namely that at the time there were 26 locomotives of the 'Merchant Navy' and 'West Country' type allocated to Nine Elms, "...which have a power rating comparable with a Deltic". How on earth this figure was arrived at cannot be imagined.

It was then stated that the steam engines covered a maximum of 24 duties with the 'Deltics' likely to replace just four steam turns and consequently saving just this same number of steam locos. How this figure was arrived at is not reported, but in so far as the flexibility and availability for work of the new machines was concerned the SR management was being nothing but ultra-conservative. Does this even mean the ER was being ultra-optimistic in its own assessment?

Whatever, the SR continued by admitting that in order to ensure maximum usage it would be necessary to use the new engines on regular daily duties although some of these would need to be double-manned: which ones and why were not stated. Accordingly it was not felt there could be any reduction in the numbers of footplate staff.

Next came the costs: each of the new locomotives was anticipated to cost £150,000, added to which were six 12-coach trains sets, five in use and one spare and of the type referred to previously. These were estimated at £12,000 per vehicle.[2] Then there were two new 12-coach Pullman sets for the 'Cunarder' and 'Statesman' workings, this time at £12,500 per car. Next so far as rolling stock was concerned were modifications to the wiring of 20 luggage vans to accommodate an electric heating circuit. Here at least the amount was nominal, a paltry £2,000. Finally came servicing needs, £20,000 for an illuminated inspection pit and special fuelling plant at Nine Elms: a grand total of £2,236,000. No allowance was made for any alterations being made at Eastleigh.

Clearly this amount of investment was seen as

Examples from the 'Special Traffic Notices for June 1957, reported as been the busiest month for Boat Trains. The names of some of the special workings are less known and it cannot be certain then that all these carried headboards.

	a.m.				UP—continued
	8 55	..	So'ton Old Docks ..	Waterloo	**Additional.** 'Nieuw Amsterdam'. Train No. B.26
	9 20	..	Weymouth .. }	Waterloo	**Run separately from Bournemouth Central to**
	10 12	..	Bournemouth West }		**Waterloo.**
	9 25	..	Bournemouth Ctl. ..	Wolverhampton	**Additional.** (Relief to 9.20 a.m. Bournemouth West). Calling at Oxford, Banbury, Leamington Spa and Birmingham.
	-9 33	..	So'ton New Docks ..	Waterloo ..	**Will convey passengers off R.M.S. 'Arundel Castle.'** Train No. B.27. 'The Union-Castle Express.'
	10 12 Q	..	Bournemouth West	Waterloo	**Will run** .. ..
	10 13	..	Southampton Term.	Reading General ..	Revised from Eastleigh .. ..
	10 55	..	So'ton New Docks ..	Waterloo	**Additional.** 'Arundel Castle'. Train No. B.28
	11 10	..	Bournemouth Ctl. ..	Sheffield	**Additional.** (Relief to 11.16 a.m. Bournemouth West). Calling at Oxford, Banbury, Rugby Central, Leicester Central, Loughborough Central and Nottingham Victoria.
	11 30	..	Weymouth .. }		
	p.m.			Waterloo	**Will run separately from Bournemouth Central to**
	12 20	..	Bournemouth West }		**Waterloo and revised.**
	12 6	..	Southampton Ctl. ..	Waterloo	**Additional Passenger** .. ..
	1 15	..	Eastleigh	Clapham Jct. ..	**Revised** .. ..
	(Parcels)				
	1 25	..	Weymouth .. }	Waterloo	**Run separately from Bournemouth Central to**
	2 20	..	Bournemouth West }		**Waterloo.**
	2 9	..	Southampton Ctl. ..	Waterloo	**Additional Passenger** .. .. ..
	2 11 Q	..	Millbrook D. Exit }	Waterloo	**Pathway not available.**
	2 15 Q	..	So'ton Dk. Gates }		
	(Boat)				
	2 20 Q	..	Bournemouth West	Waterloo	**Will run** .. ..
	3 50	..	Weymouth .. }	Waterloo	**Run separately Bournemouth Central to Waterloo.**
	5 5	..	Bournemouth West }		3.50 p.m. Weymouth will leave Bournemouth Central 5.9 p.m. and run to Q timing.
	4 12	..	Southampton Ctl. ..	Waterloo	**Additional Passenger** .. .. ..
	4 15	..	Bournemouth West	Waterloo	**Additional Passenger** .. .. ..
	4‖23	..	Lymington Pier ..	Brockenhurst ..	**Will not run.** .. .. ..
	5 9 Q	..	Bournemouth Ctl. ..	Waterloo	**Will run.** Formed of 3.50 p.m. ex Weymouth. ..
	5 23	..	Southampton Term.	Alton..	**Revised** .. ..
	5 30	..	Southampton Docks	Waterloo	Pass Northam Jct. 5.40 p.m. and run 1 minute later thence.
	5 35	..	Weymouth .. }	Waterloo	**Revised.** Will run separately from Bournemouth
	6 16	..	Bournemouth West }		**Central to Waterloo.**
	6 16	..	Bournemouth West	Waterloo	**Revised from Bournemouth Central** .. ..
	6 30	..	Swanage	Wareham	Start 6.40 p.m. and run 10 minutes later thence ..
	6‖30	..	Christchurch ..	Brockenhurst ..	**Start** 6‖52 p.m. and **revised** .. .. ..
	6 56	..	Southampton Term.	Alton	Arrive Shawford 7.22 p.m., depart 7.23 p.m., arrive Winchester City 7.29 p.m., depart 7.32 p.m. pass Winchester Jct. 7.38 p.m. and run 4 minutes later to Alresford and 2 minutes later thence.
	7 48	..	Weymouth ..	Reading General ..	Depart Brockenhurst 10.6 p.m. and run 2 minutes later to Southampton Central.
	9 18	..	Swanage	Wareham	Start 9.25 p.m. and **revised** .. .. ..

Headboard-less, but clearly from the Pullman formation this was an important working. No. 30850 in charge of the up 'Royal Mail Lines' boat-train running on the up through line just south of Shawford. 16th August 1958.

Tony Molyneaux / KR Collection

unrealistic from the outset, although the obvious palliative of charging a supplement to passengers on the Ocean Liner services was quickly rejected as it was pointed out these unfortunates were already being fleeced (*this was not the word used in the report*) at higher rates than ordinary passengers, 50% extra in first-class and 35% extra in second-class. It was what in more recent times might be regarded as a 'Catch 22' situation, Waterloo recognising the need to afford, "an improved standard of service", yet unable to do so despite the receipts obtained yielding "a good profit margin". Indeed the cost of running any of the Ocean Liner workings was seen to be just £119 per trip, with a hoped for minimum return of £160 per train equivalent to £200,000 per annum. This total had been comfortably exceeded in both 1956 and 1957, the totals being £276,229 and £266,808 respectively, equivalent to a return of £221 and £213 per train over the two years.

From what was clearly a confidential report it is apparent there was also a degree of greed by the operators, for Passengers Excess Luggage charges totalled £19,976 in 1956 and £16,929 in 1957. These amounts are included in the figures quoted.

By their very nature, the trouble with the Ocean Liner specials was that their departure times from Southampton could vary considerably due to the vagaries of weather and tides. As such the operators had always to allow for as many 'Q' paths as possible in the up direction but it was admitted that some of these afforded limited opportunity to achieve the desired 80 minute schedule. Train running in some of the 'Q' paths also meant consequential alteration to regular freight workings. Operating a limited diesel scheme would also mean providing two separate 'Q' paths per train, one timed for steam and the other for diesel haulage.

In 1958 the rolling stock situation used for the boat trains came from a pool of 90 vehicles, all of which were carefully selected and serviced for what were regarded as prestige workings. The actual consist being five eight-coach sets, from a pool of five First-Brake vehicles, 20 First Class, and 25 Open-Second. With new stock, 50 of the above would be considered redundant including 18 Pullman cars which were normally set aside specifically for the Ocean liner workings. The remaining 40 vehicles would be relegated to replace the then present day spare stock currently used to supplement on peak days. No savings were anticipated relative to the converted luggage vans, indeed it may even have been that some difficulty would be created in this area, for it would be necessary to ensure the specially fitted vehicles were always available, compared with the present arrangements where vans came from a common pool.

The report concluded with the potential for use of the 'Deltics' post-Electrification. At the time the only potential was seen as being on the Salisbury and Exeter services although curiously there is still mention of a Waterloo – Weymouth diesel service. Perhaps Bournemouth to Weymouth would be a shuttle working with a few separate loco-hauled through workings from Waterloo?

"If and when electrification is extended to Exeter it would be difficult to find economic use for this class on the Region". So read the penultimate paragraph of the report, an added rider being, "A similar position would apply in respect of the special coaching stock if it were decided to run electric multiple-unit trains between Waterloo and Southampton Docks."

As such the final conclusions were obvious. C P Hopkins, the Southern Region General Manager, was unable to recommend either the new locomotives or modern rolling stock. One wonders though if this was in effect a paper exercise, made to fit what was already a foregone conclusion. Credence for this comes in the comment on the number of steam locomotives the new diesels would have been likely to replace. Utilisation of

34072 ' 257 Squadron' coming back on shed at Eastleigh having worked the down 'Cunarder' service. The variation in headboard shape compared with the illustration on page 72 will be noted.

Equally important to the Boat Train services were the ECS workings. Top is No. 34036 passing Allbrook at 6.48 pm on 29th August 1963 with empty boat train stock. Below, it is the turn of an unidentified 'U' hauling 'blood and custard' Bulleid stock away from the Western Docks at Southampton in late spring / early summer of 1955. When out of use, coaching stock for the special workings was held mainly at Clapham junction or in the Docks themselves. Perhaps the best option of all might not have been to consider new motive power but simply to concentrate resources on improvements to the existing rolling stock on its own. As we now know, there was to be little change to either locomotives or coaching stock for these workings at all.

Tony Molyneaux / KR collection.

modern motive power in the report was perhaps a slightly strange issue. The Southern Region were already well-versed in interspersing steam and electric traction, seemingly without undue delays to either, and the flexibility afforded by diesel seems to have been overlooked. The experience of years earlier with 10201 and her sisters and their ability to regain time had clearly been forgotten.

History would, of course, record it was also the right decision, perhaps not for the passengers but certainly as far as raw economics were concerned. In the event, circumstances outside the control of the railways were to play a part, with a change from ocean to air travel so far as the long-distance travelling public were concerned. Boat trains and Ocean Liner specials would indeed continue to form a part of the scene right through until July 1967, but then, like the steam engine,

they seemed to fade away, the final workings often in the hands of the converted Class 74 electro-diesel type at the head of ordinary stock. So far as what might have been the future use for any 'Deltic' locomotive post-1967, here the answer is simple: the SR could well have continued to operate a locomotive-hauled Pullman service if required, a modern day 'Bournemouth Belle' perhaps. Certainly a 'Deltic' would have been able to maintain the necessary speeds involved to intermingle with the regular electric workings. But that was not to be. The fact the Southern Region resisted what was in effect an interim dieselisation programme is understandable. also as witness the visual effect this may have had to ordinary travellers forced to endure an 'old-fashioned' steam service. Had there been a fleet of engines on the region and had they indeed been made redundant post-1967 then there could have been use elsewhere, not perhaps on the Southern but certainly elsewhere on BR, the Midland line out of St Pancras being the obvious example. Save for when working railtours, there has never been any regular 'Deltic' working on the SR, and the fact the 'Deltic' design not only lived up to but exceeded the expectations of the operators at Kings Cross for two decades was a tribute to the design.

1. Conversation between retired Loco Inspector Mark Abbott and the author on the basis of notes made by Mark Abbott at Nine Elms in 1966. At this time withdrawals of the MN class had escalated to such an extent that official notification had been given to the loco inspectors that this transfer was likely to take place in the near future.

2. An appended note commented that: "It is estimated that to afford significant improvement over present standards of accommodation the cost of luxury coaches would be between £12,000 and £15,000 each. The compares with £8,000 - £10,000 for a BR Standard main-line coach.

There does not appear to be any evidence that the SR or LMS main-line diesel locos were ever used on OLE workings, although other than rostering issues, there was certainly no reason why they might not have been. (LMS 10000 seen here at Surbiton in July 1953 with a Salisbury to Waterloo semi-fast). The year when the Deltic issue was being discussed, 1957, was also the time when the SR seemed intent on seeing dieselisation as the way forward with the introduction of the Hastings and Hampshire DEMU sets. Consider also that even with diesel seen as a thought for the future, still to come was the rebuilding of numerous Bulleid Pacifics in the post 1958 period. Might the cost of main line dieselisation have been considerably reduced if the rebuilding plan had not gone ahead? Indeed as recorded in the text even in 1957 it was anticipated steam would be gone within a decade. We do not know if the WR were similarly invited to make a case for Deltics. Was it even that this situation had been forced on the SR on the basis that a multiple order might reduce costs: it might even have been that BRB had been seduced by the performance of the prototype Deltic and sought to convince the regions that they could all benefit, certainly it would appear the SR did little to create a strong case for use out of Waterloo.   *Arthur Tayler / KR Collection*

Terry Cole's Rolling Stock File No. 9
'Three 3s'

The Southern Railway was very organised with regard to its passenger services, running the majority of its coaches in fixed formation sets. The same coaches would run together for years, sometimes even from construction to withdrawal, and if one coach required attention the whole set would be stopped and replaced by another of the same type. Whereas electric stock formations were latterly 2s, 4s, or 6s, (apart from the Brighton Belle), 3 coaches was probably the most common set formation for steam stock, certainly in the later Southern and BR(S) periods.

At busy times trains would be strengthened by adding additional 'loose' coaches at the front or rear or by using two sets instead of one.

Opposite top - C2X No. 32546 is seen near Ashurst Junction on 13 September 1950 with an East Grinstead to Tunbridge Wells West train formed of an ex-SECR 3 coach 'Birdcage' set. This is one of 62 Trio Type C sets of 60ft stock built from 1912 which, when built, were the longest coaches running on any of the Southern's constituent companies. The leading vehicle is an 8-compartment 3rd brake to SR diagram 160 (SR numbers 3404 -3465) seating 80 third class passengers. The rear vehicle was formerly a 2nd / 3rd lavatory composite now downgraded to all-third and seating 54. It is to SR diagram 162 (SR numbers 3476 - 3537) with 7 compartments, a corridor 2 compartments long on each side giving 4 compartments access to a lavatory. In the centre is a saloon composite (originally 2nd / 3rd) to SR Diagram 315/6 seating 26 first and 30 third class passengers (SR numbers 5433 – 5493). The sets remained largely unchanged and were withdrawn between 1954 and 1958. Together with the other SECR 3-coach Birdcage sets they saw widespread use not only on the ex-SECR lines but also on ex-LBSCR lines east of the Brighton main line.

Opposite bottom - L1 No. 31759 enters Tonbridge with a down local train on 25 June 1952 formed of Maunsell restriction '0'set 941 and two southern 'vans'. This is one of nine 3-coach sets built for the Hastings line in 1934 and were the last vehicles built for that line before the 'Hastings DMUs' of the late 1950s. Originally the sets were intended to have a 'typical' 3-car formation of a composite flanked by two brake thirds. However in the 1930s first class numbers had declined, so they were built with two brake composites either side of a full corridor third. The brake compos are 6881 and 6882 to diagram 2402 and the third 1038 to diagram 2004. Being only 8ft wide fewer seats were possible, so the whole set capacity was only 16 1st and 96 3rd. Known as 'O' sets in working notices they sometimes ran with additional loose vehicles, even Pullman cars, added *inside* the sets. They were refurbished from 1952 onwards, and this particular set was withdrawn in September 1959.

This page - Here we see the final development of Southern coaching stock downgraded to branch line use. Bulleid 3-coach set 90 waits to leave West Grinstead with a Horsham-Brighton train c1964. Originally built in 1949 as a 4-coach set for the London-Dover-Margate services it was one of the first Bulleid sets to incorporate the deeper 15in ventilators as well as being one of the last to be out-shopped in malachite green. In 1963 it was reduced to 3 coaches and used on Central Section branch line services. Semi-open brake thirds (now 2nds) 4031 and 4032 flank corridor composite 5833 in a typical 3 set formation to give 24 1st and 110 3rd (2nd) seats. It ended its days with the final steam services on the SW section. [All photos Terry Cole collection]

One of the pleasures in compiling 'SW' is the feedback received. Speaking as a mere mortal there is some consolation in knowing it is not just the editor who gets it wrong sometimes, but more importantly there really is a wealth of expertise and knowledge out these which people are so willing to share.

Firstly going back to Issue No 6, we asked the question if anyone could identify the motorcycle in the view of the bridge at Hedge Corner. David Austin came up trumps here courtesy of the HMVF forum; "The motorcycle is a Norton 16H, WD 16H C383081, supplied under contract C9681 which commenced delivery in March 1937. Originally for 1,790 machines with a census number beginning C373731, it was extended to 2,222 motorcycles, the last of these being delivered, as far as I can see from the factory ledgers, during the early part of 1938. These early machines carried no sump guard or pillion equipment and this one has the characteristic large Ni-Fe (Nickel Iron) battery which was specified for WD Nortons pre-war. Genuine pre-war WD Nortons are a rarity now as the vast majority of them went to France with the regular units of the BEF."

Next we come to Jeffrey Grayer's 'Scuppering the 'U' Boats' article, from 'SW7', which brought back specific memories to Keith Widdowson. "My 'Iron Horse' chasing started in earnest during the summer of 64 and having 'discovered' a ready supply of new steam catches from a multitude of classes operating trains over the Reading to Redhill route decided, upon learning of their imminent demise, to blitz the route during the final two months of that year. During that period I caught 2 x Manors, 2 x Q1s, 8 x Ns, 6 x Us, 4 x 73xxx, 3 x 76xxx

Two views of the 'Bournemouth Limited' kindly submitted by Barry Sillance and we believe originally from the camera of the late S C Townroe. The location is probably near Christchurch. This train commenced operation in July 1929 and was initially the province of 'Lord Nelson' and later 'King Arthur' class engines. 'Schools' class locos, in what was originally known as the new 'Bournemouth Green' livery, officially 'Malachite', began working the service from 1937, consequent upon their being displaced from the Portsmouth line following electrification. Despite being the smallest of the three loco types referred to, the 'Schools' were well suited to the task, even when the loading increased to 12 vehicles. (A 3-coach set for Weymouth, 2-coach set off the Swanage branch, and a 6-coach Restaurant Car set fro Bournemouth West, the latter on occasions augmented by an additional loose corridor–third.) All the vehicles allocated to the duty were similarly bedecked in the new external livery whilst internally 'rexine' cloth was used with the seats also having individual backs and a revised compartment décor featuring scenes rather than advertising.

and 5 x 80xxx. Positioning myself at Guildford suitably equipped with Privilege return tickets to both Gomshall and Wanborough, I was able to hop on and off services dependent upon my needs. Comparing Jeffrey's list of the final 22 Mogul's that made it into 1965. I note with some satisfaction that of the 8 'missed' for haulage only one (31803) escaped my camera (some of which are featured on my growing collection on John Bird's www.southern-images.co.uk website). Away from the line Jeffrey mentions the 07.30 Woking to Basingstoke service, but alas every time I went for it, a 'Standard 5' was always the power. The 15.12 Basingstoke to Woking stopper was caught in August 64 and instead of the expected 'S15' I collected a run with Guildford's 31858 - being disappointed at the time! Not always one for 'spotting', I did however sometimes make notes if something out of the ordinary was seen and to this end, taking into account the diminishing Mogul numbers, they qualified for such an entry. 31873 worked out of Waterloo with the 19.54 service to Basingstoke on 19/05/65. On 11/12/65 31639 was on a Down Parcels at Brookwood and 31809 on a ballast at Farnborough. On 09/02/66 31405 & 31639 were seen at Woking and excepting the two railtours I was on, (03/04 & 30/04), my final sighting of the class was 31791 on a Parcels at Woking on 04/05/66. Courtesy of the magnificent work performed by the Preservation societies my tally of Mogul haulages has risen from the end of steam total of 17 to a current high of 22. Keep up the excellent quality of Southern Way - I have just renewed my subscription." - *well, I had to leave that last bit in!*

Now bang up to date reference both 'SW7' and

The two-hour timing, non-stop between Waterloo and Bournemouth in either direction, was not particularly fast, but this included the severe slack around Northam curve and a consideration that the engine should not work unduly hard so the tender water supplies would be sufficient. If trouble did occur in this area it would undoubtedly be on the up working, due to the gradients involved north of Eastleigh. The 'Bournemouth Limited' was one of the few services to have omitted a stop at Southampton and continued as such for a decade until curtailed on 9 September 1939. Subsequent to this, a revised service operated in a similar timetable path, 8.40 am up from Bournemouth and 4.35 pm down from Waterloo; the 'Limited' had departed at 4.30 pm. The revised train bore no name and also added stops at Winchester and Southampton. Post war, in 1951, the new 'Royal Wessex' service took over an almost identical slot in the timetable although now with regular intermediate stops at Winchester, Southampton and Brockenhurst. The original destinations, each having a separate coach portion, viz, Bournemouth West, Swanage and Weymouth, were maintained.

'SW8' from Neil Knowlden, "I KNEW there was something to comment on from SW7 when I bought SW8 from you yesterday .... and now I've remembered what it was ! - a minor point to most people, maybe, but the ballast cleaning photo sequence was most definitely NOT taken in South London - Petts Wood was still firmly in <u>Kent</u> at that time (and, geographically, that's where it remains !) Incidentally, this looks like the Up loop from St.Mary Cray to Chislehurst - hence it's single track though it connects the Chatham Line (two-track in those days) to the four-track South Eastern main line that crosses overhead. (Autobiographical Note 1 : pictures taken the month before I was born.)

Alan Postlethwaite's fascinating article on St.Johns station certainly clarified a few aspects of this place that had always intrigued me - though still leaving one or two oddities to be explained by others ! (Please). Alan is quite right listing the train lengths that can be seen at St.Johns but - as an 'expatriate' - he may not be aware that the 12-car sets will all be through workings on the fast lines. Though most of the platforms in the area were, indeed, lengthened for twelve coaches, many years ago now, the local services normally only see 4, 5, 8 or 10 cars - that's one or two Networkers or one or two Cattle Trucks - sorry, Class 376 Electrostars. The two-car Networkers (466) do put in the occasional appearance to make a six-set but I've not seen a 4 + 4 + 2 formation - on the Mid Kent at least - for ages. (Dartford & Orpington lines may be different.) It's ironic that the current scene railway press frequently talk about double-deck trains (now there's an idea Mr.Bulleid) to increase capacity when all these platform extensions lie idle: I surmise that the St.Johns Vale Road bridge was rebuilt solely to give room for the extension here - what a waste of money - and life.

Alan refers to the coal traffic from Erith to Catford travelling the great way round (no caps) via Tonbridge rather than reversing at St.Johns. At about the time of Nationalisation, all this traffic seems to have run via Blackheath and some did actually did reverse at St.Johns although most climbed the hill to Brockley to run round - I only have the one WTT so cannot say how long-lived this arrangement was. (Transcript attached - *sorry, space constraints - Ed.*)
(Autobiographical Note 2 : As I was reading Alan's article I was thinking of commenting on my father's lucky escape by catching an earlier train on the day of the Lewisham / St.Johns smash : as Alan says - in more or less the words I was going to use - they 'and a thousand others .... were lucky' .... others were not so fortunate.)"

Now additional information from Stephen Grant over the view which appeared on P94 of 'SW7'. "My guess would be that Les Duffel's picture of the 5-Bel unit passing through Liphook was taken on 14 April 1954 when unit 3052 took the young Prince Charles and Princess Anne from Waterloo to Portsmouth to board the newly-commissioned Royal Yacht 'Britannia' for a voyage to Tobruk to be reunited with their parents who were returning from a three-month Royal tour of Australia. According to Julian Morel, then a senior officer of the Pullman Car Company, Prince Charles was surprised by the absence of a locomotive and enquired whether there was a man at the front. During the journey he and Princess Anne were taken through the train to meet the motorman.

The headcode (07) indicates a non-stop run from Waterloo to Portsmouth & Southsea, which was presumably a more convenient location than the Harbour station if 'Britannia' was berthed in the naval dockyards."

We have received some additional material from Stephen Duffell, who contributed the view of what was believed to be a 5-BEL* set (see caption note) passing Liphook and attributed to Les Duffell. Stephen has sent some most interesting views and biographical details of his uncle's career on the Southern.

*Colin Chivers kindly loaned us this image of unit 3052 at Waterloo from the camera of the late Denis Cullum. The view was taken on 20 July 1951 although it cannot be as was suggested for the Naval review as this was in June 1953. * Tony Logan has drawn our attention to the fact that on the occasion of the working seen at Liphook, an extra Pullman coach had been added, thus making in effect a temporary 6-BEL set.*

'REBUILDING'-THE LETTERS AND COMMENTS PAGE(S)

FROM A RAILWAYMAN'S FAMILY PHOTO ALBUM

Les Duffell, (Jack Leslie Duffell 1912-1994), was a railwayman, employed first by the Southern Railway and later British Railways (Southern Region). Born in Earlsfield, SW London, in the family photo albums there are a few views illustrating his career, that began in 1926 as a 'Messenger boy' at Waterloo Station. From 1928-1935 he was a porter at Berrylands Station.

Surbiton Station Master (Mr Butler) with the traffic cash bag collected at Berry-lands 1934.

Standing in the four foot was the place to be photographed! Sid Todd (porter) Berrylands 1934.

Not all pictures were taken on the track. Berrylands station 1934 with, (left to right), Porter Jim Alvis, Girl from tobacco kiosk, man from electric depot, Porter Sid Todd.

From 1935-38 Les was a porter at Yarmouth on the Isle of Wight, where the Southern Railway had a small railway station and the ferry terminal for the Lymington to Yarmouth service. Presumably the staff were expected to work at either site? Did porters have to transfer goods and passenger luggage between the quay and station? (Yarmouth Station is seen in the mid 1930s.)

In 1938 Les married a girl from the Isle of Wight and they moved to the Haslemere area where he got a job as a porter at Liphook station. He was also a shunter and during the war a member of the Home Guard.

Centre - Les is seen on the left.

Clearly it was not all work! 'High Jinks' on Yarmouth Quay, mid 1930s. In the top angled view, Les is on the right, in the bottom angled view, he is seen on the left. The lady is not identified.

In 1950 Les became a Booking Clerk at Liphook station and in 1960 Chief Booking Clerk at Haslemere. In 1976 he received a certificate and gift for 50 years service to the Railways. He retired in 1977.

Left second from bottom - Shunting Haslemere yard (upside) – shunter Arthur Hooker. Locomotive No. 2060, an ex-LBSCR B4X. Late 1940s.
Left bottom - Les Duffell and uniformed porter at Liphook station in the 1960s when Les was Chief Booking Clerk at Haslemere, but covered some duties at Liphook.
Angled view right - Liphook 1960. Station staff with certificate for First Prize (?best kept station?). Les Duffell second from left. Station Master R H Croydon.

What better way to conclude this section than with a 1930s view of the Isle of Wight car ferry at Fishbourne. (It should of course be Yarmouth really).

We regret that pressure on space means several appreciated items of correspondence have had to be held over to next time. With grateful thanks (and in no particular order) to Bill Jackson - re additional information on the Callington Branch, John Davenport - re Clapham Junction signal box collapse, Colin Hall - also on the Clapham Signal box collapse, M J Harvey - re Clapham Junction Signal School, Alan Morris - re the picture of Scammell lorry in Issue 2, Eric Penn - re the image of Waterloo on page 2 of Issue 7, Roger Macdonald, re Horsted Keynes and 'Invincible', and last but by no means least, Eric Best re Clapham Junction.

Full details of these, and no doubt additional correspondence, will appear in Issue 10.

THE DAILY EXPRESS, AUGUST 7, 1922.

DO BE CAREFUL, DRIVER.

HERO WORSHIP.

Children always look forward to the railway journey to the seaside, with the mystery of the locomotive, its driver, and the long steel track that leads to pleasures new.

Permanent Way Notes by Graham Hatton

Track design and its Evolution

Over this series of articles so far I have looked at many aspects of construction work associated with the permanent way: now I will have a look at the work of the drawing office behind actual track work for the two principal areas, plain line and switch and crossing, and focus on how standards evolved through natural development and how they are used.

The importance and usage of standards.

'Rules are for the obedience of the people and for the guidance of wise men'. The railways have always been and will always be a good example of the need for a disciplined approach to construction aspects within the world of permanent way and many of its related fields, such as signalling and electrification. Roman engineers had an established set of standards for the construction of the roads which linked the provinces of their empire, and provided the means of communication to tell the troops what was expected of them far from Rome, and this standardisation is one of the earliest examples of what can be achieved when constructing on a massive scale, just as the early railways did. As far as railways were concerned 'standards' were set down to ensure each railway was built to a common set of values but they were not exactly the same for neighbouring companies! A good example is the GWR and LSWR; clearly the Broad Gauge had much larger structural clearances and after its demise this allowed more generous clearances to remain, such as wide six-foots and better platform clearances. Some GWR tunnels seem like cathedrals when compared with those of its close neighbour the LSWR! Even within the Southern Region, the three principal companies at the grouping were still constrained by differing standards for construction.

In many cases early standards were in effect 'best practice', but to ensure local interpretation was kept to an acceptable and controlled level most of these items became more formalised instructions or standards.

In the beginning track was very primitive and the early engineers had little previous knowledge to guide them. Once the 'temporary way,' the light and often repositioned construction track used during the building process was removed, the 'permanent way' could be laid. It is not permanent as in for ever, merely

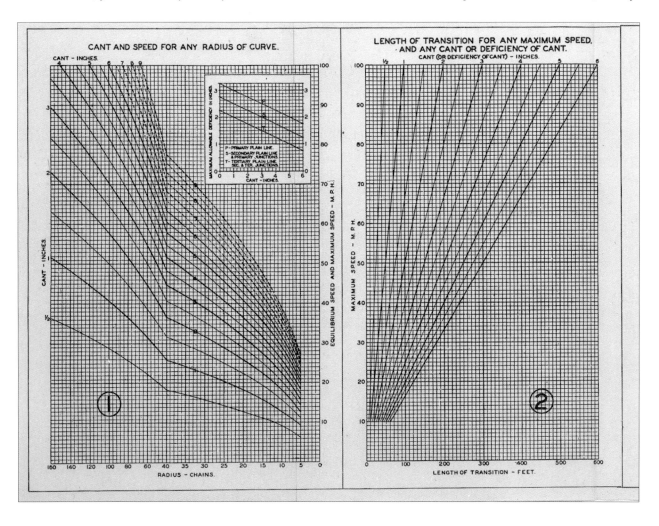

lasting an average of 30 years or so, but it's the intention that this track is not frequently repositioned, requiring no more than normal maintenance during its lifetime. To ensure the permanent way was consistent, it quickly acquired a host of supporting standards, largely derived from experience gained, which were printed for the purpose of building successive track to an equal or better standard.

The need to establish the spacing of tracks to ensure trains passed safely illustrates the need for a consistent approach to construction. Six-foots were very often tighter than the exact measurement, and then the loading gauge of the trains needed to be checked to ensure that although the six-foot measurement was infringed the trains

A 1904 SE&CR chair in Sandown yard IOW. Still there and although hardly ever run on, technically still in service! It is actually on the end of a genuine, largely LSWR turnout, still with many original but long since superseded items.

still passed each other with safe clearances. Where standards were not met this could result in real problems. For example on the Hastings route the Southern was saddled with a whole host of 'restricted route clearance' stock for this route and a lack of freedom of movement until the line was singled, in recent years, through the very tight tunnels.

Of course most of these standards have been rewritten over the years, but in many cases the standards have simply been enhanced to give even more information and hence guidance on the 'current' company policies.

After the initial trials of many railway companies, each realised the need for, and evolved a set of, company standards in written and drawing format. Many of these were also the result of the Inspecting Railway Officer's requirements and they are often spoken of in the formal reports into the opening of new railway lines. So, for instance, rail lengths, sleeper spacing, ballast suitability, platform construction - particularly height, width and spacing, and the structure clearances for bridges and tunnels, were all standardised; but not, unfortunately to any common value until the First World War. Then, under the Railway Executive Committee (REC) and its associated Engineering Association (REA), the need to standardise across the whole railway system on minimum acceptable standards for greater flexibility of train movements was tackled. The Southern Railway duly wrote their set of standards soon after

the 'grouping' in 1923, though work had started before that date. Similarly, the other members of the big four produced their drawings to support the REA standards, though individuality of detail in these drawings still persisted for some items such as rail chairs etc.

To this day much of this standardisation to the REA standards is still used and published under the Permanent Way Institution's (PWI) documents and referred to in the set of accompanying standard drawings. Many modern permanent way designs are simply an extension of this system.

The development of plain line standards

To illustrate plain line I will use the LSWR which had a typically evolved background to permanent way. Early track used 50lb, 15ft lengths in 1850. By the late 1880s this had become 82lb in 24ft lengths. Both were wrought iron and double headed, that is to say they had the same head and foot in the mistaken belief they could be turned over and give further life. In reality the rail foot wore in the chair and gave a very uneven surface (called rail gall), the rail surface being stepped down where every chair had worn it. Even 1/16" or 1/8" "regularly indented on a rail head will give a noisy and poor ride and lead to increased rail failure. By 1886 it had become steel rail, which is much stronger and by the 1890s the rail length had increased to 30ft with the first references to BH rail which has the distinctive larger head section.

July 1957, site unknown, but taken, presumably again to illustrate FB jointed Heyback track with a good line and top. This may be after recent mechanised maintenance as the ballast is clearly lower in the areas immediately either side of the rail illustrating these areas have been packed whereas the centre of the sleeper does not require packing. Also of note is the cabling hung on the adjacent concrete posts and metal support brackets. The actual cable is a High Voltage sub-station link cable and the big box on the cable on the right contains an HV cable joint. These are, not surprisingly, complex joints, which take considerable skill and time to make, employing specialist staff. The cable also sits on short lengths of wood boarding in the bracket to prevent attrition of the cable sheathing with expansion movement.

The standards of the 1890s issued to the work force were that each 30ft length should contain 11 sleepers, 9"x 10" x 5", whereas earlier sleepers in between the joint sleepers were half round (half a tree!). The sleepers would be equally spaced, but joint sleepers would be 1'1" from the rail end to their centre, a common and long-lasting dimension.

Some companies, such as the SECR, experimented with fully-supported joints. These were joints where the sleeper is under the actual joint and the fishplate and chair are one. However most companies used the normal 'suspended' joints between sleepers.

By 1902 90lb rail was being used, and 12 sleepers per 30ft with the tighter joint spacing of sleepers as above. By 1903 the company had sourced 45 ft rails and this remained standard till the grouping. Note that LSWR rail was always 2 ½ inches head width; British Standard BH rail is 2 ¾ inches head width.

As railway companies sourced rail from outside manufacturing companies and these companies were in competition to sell their products, it seems sensible to assume that the rail sizes and lengths, although uniquely rolled for each company, probably developed to similar timescales in other railway companies.

60ft rails came at about the same time as the grouping, but of course actually took years of normal track renewals to introduce generally and many secondary routes and sidings even now retain the slightly shorter rails.

The companies were at least all clear on the need for expansion joints! Those for the Engineering Department of the LSWR are shown in the extract.

After initial problems due to simple lack of experience, track lasted for many years in most locations, and in some areas many decades, so mixed styles of track are common. Some early railway companies like those who owned the Circle Line in London initially had to learn the hard way about the most suitable style of rail, most of their track was relaid twice in about 15 years due to experience gained from track damage! The length of a track's life is affected by its usage and its location. The first is obvious, the second less so. An example of the importance of the latter is the tunnel. These are often damp, sometimes just wet! This has a huge impact on the speed of corrosion and attrition of the rail surface. A wet tunnel location can shorten the life of even modern steel rails to, say, 7 years.

Having set its standards for track the LSWR updated these as the years passed and it issued these to the various Inspectors to keep their track to the latest standard when undertaking renewals. Slavish adherence was not usually measured by rule, but men understood the need to comply in principle even though they did not always understand the reasoning! So slight variations in sleeper spacing were normal; the correct number per length in very nearly the correct position and more importantly, supporting any joint correctly were what the wiser men knew they had to achieve. Again, sleepers can be pulled through (moved sideways by a few inches) and rebored to renew the chairscrew fixing, so sleeper ends are not always in absolute line! Some rails would inevitably be shorter than the standard, but again tolerances were often specified (as they still are) of just how short rails could be! Similarly the track needed to be canted and curved in accordance with set guide lines. Here early experience soon gave way to a more mathematical approach as speeds increased.

As speeds were generally low, much early track was mainly laid as simple curves and straights. Transitions, the method of moving from one radius - often straight track (of infinite radius in mathematical terms) to a curved radius over a set distance, or from one curved radius to another, caused unduly rough rides. Mid range radii were tried by some companies, but the transition first propounded by Froude in about 1860 was developed by others, especially Shortt of the LSWR, into a practical system along with the rules applying to curves and cant, and a graphical method of designing curves from versines (the offset at the middle of overlapping chords measured along the track at equal distances). The original track being set out by mathematical offsets and the use of theodolites for alignment is still used, but is more involved than the versine method.

Shortt's system is still in use in drawing offices and although other systems, such as that derived by Hallade, using number tables, are similar, all form the basis

Below - *Clapham Junction, July 1957. In the foreground the Down Brighton Fast line is laid with FB jointed Heyback baseplates and fastenings. These are effectively a flattened spring clip, but in time through wear and age they loose there grip. Of note is the 'flow' of the curve and the slight applied cant or crosslevel. The rolled steel baseplates are secured by lockspikes to the sleepers, the loops of which can be seen above the baseplate. Lockspikes are no more than a large split pin driven into a bored hole. In time they were less effective than screws. The adjacent BH. Up Fast line on the left has slightly different construction here using longitudinal timbers and transoms. At this point all lines pass over Falcon Road underbridge. This diversity of track types over underbridges usually through renewal is not uncommon. To the left is the end of the SW, 'A' Signal Box, featured in Southern Way No 7. To the right is the Brighton Line Signal Box.*

of systems which are simply computerised in their output today. though the old habits die hard and Shortt's remained the preferred SW system till recently!

Given the radius and speed, by these systems it then became possible to quantify accurately the amount of cant to apply to curves and how this should be 'run up' at each end, without knowing all the supporting mathematics! This running up of cant at the same location as the transition amounted to twisting the track both vertically for the cant and horizontally for the radii within allowable limits.

Again this can be calculated precisely, and certainly by 1909 when Shortt and Spiller produced papers on the subject there was clear maths to support their theories. However again it is not quite as simple as that and local engineers and inspectors knew when things might need to be 'tweaked' to achieve a better result. For instance the amount of cant applied to the curve is varied according to the speed, but running a mixed traffic area would require an average speed to be canted for, so some trains ran faster than the curve was canted for and 'rode or wore' the high rail and vice versa. In time this too became a standard and has allowable tolerances now, but for the man on the ground, his Inspector would often, in consultation with an Engineer, vary such standards to overcome rail sidewear, for instance. All companies published literature for the basis of the requirements.

Cant was normally marked out in steps of ½" though the values below are precise calculated values.

Chains	Max Speed	Cant (Inches)	Check Rail?
8	20	2 ¾	Yes - if for pass use.
20	20	1 ¾	
20	40	4 ¾	
40	40	2 ½	
40	60	5 ½	

So some typical values might be as follows, (radius shown in chains - 22yds/ approx 20m):-

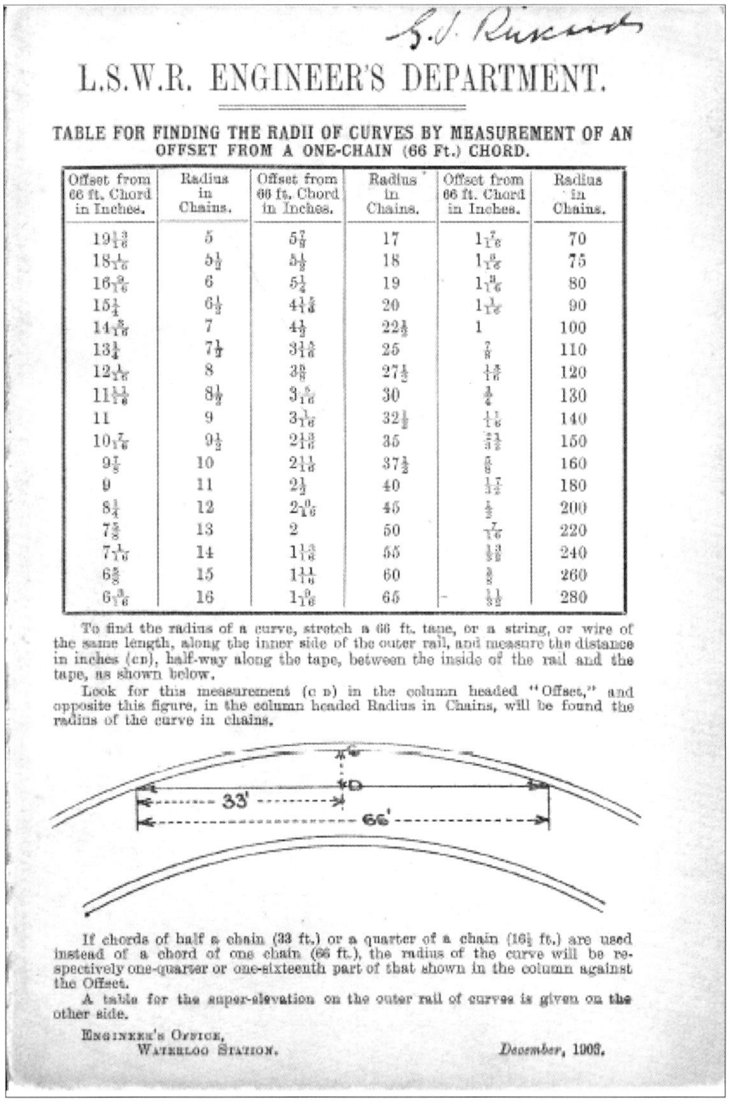

With this information and the knowledge of the radii the Inspector could adjust cant and the Ganger could check it on site or by reference to tables or site markers without the need to understand the mathematics.

When I started and an old engineer was explaining on a training course about curves, he found the best way was to relate the shape to something tangible. He suggested (approximately!) that good track should 'flow' from one curve to another rather like a lady's shape! Not p.c. perhaps, but it is true that if the track looks good in shape it will probably ride well. Smooth curves and transitions from one to another are critical, helping to 'support' the eye of the Ganger who could see where the faults lay between the areas of correct geometry. All companies used transitions from at least the turn of the last century. Similar tables were derived for rail lengths on curves to allow for the advancement of the inside rail around a curve and when to insert a shortened rail etc.

The early Inspector would have had company standards, but by the beginning of the Southern Railway the Permanent Way Inspector had the help of practical guides issued by the PWI and others, the first of which appeared in 1922. This was literally a guide to all of the accumulated knowledge at that stage and dovetailed into much of the work of the REA. Standard dimensions for such items as clearances, spaces for water columns between tracks (11'0"), standards of turntable sizes at this time (65'0"), width and depth of engine pits (3'9" x 3'0" outside), centre of buffer beam above

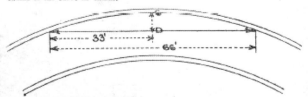

L.S.W.R. ENGINEER'S DEPARTMENT.

TABLE FOR FINDING THE RADII OF CURVES BY MEASUREMENT OF AN OFFSET FROM A ONE-CHAIN (66 Ft.) CHORD.

Offset from 66 ft. Chord in Inches.	Radius in Chains.	Offset from 66 ft. Chord in Inches.	Radius in Chains.	Offset from 66 ft. Chord in Inches.	Radius in Chains.
19¹³⁄₁₆	5	5⅞	17	1¹⁄₁₆	70
18¹⁄₁₆	5½	5⅔	18	1¹⁄₁₆	75
16⁷⁄₁₆	6	5¼	19	1¹⁄₁₆	80
15¼	6½	4¹¹⁄₁₆	20	1¹⁄₁₆	90
14⁷⁄₁₆	7	4½	22½	1	100
13¼	7½	3¹⁵⁄₁₆	25	⅞	110
12⁵⁄₁₆	8	3⅝	27½	¹⁵⁄₁₆	120
11⅜	8½	3³⁄₁₆	30	¾	130
11	9	3¹⁄₁₆	32½	¹¹⁄₁₆	140
10⁷⁄₁₆	9½	2¹³⁄₁₆	35	⁵¹⁄₃₂	150
9½	10	2¹¹⁄₁₆	37½	⅝	160
9	11	2½	40	¹¹⁄₁₆	180
8¼	12	2⁰⁄₁₆	45	½	200
7⅝	13	2	50	⁷⁄₁₆	220
7¹⁄₁₆	14	1¹³⁄₁₆	55	⁷⁄₁₆	240
6⅝	15	1¹¹⁄₁₆	60	⅜	260
6⁹⁄₁₆	16	1⁹⁄₁₆	65	¹¹⁄₃₂	280

To find the radius of a curve, stretch a 66 ft. tape, or a string, or wire of the same length, along the inner side of the outer rail, and measure the distance in inches (c D), half-way along the tape, between the inside of the rail and the tape, as shown below.

Look for this measurement (c D) in the column headed "Offset," and opposite this figure, in the column headed Radius in Chains, will be found the radius of the curve in chains.

If chords of half a chain (33 ft.) or a quarter of a chain (16½ ft.) are used instead of a chord of one chain (66 ft.), the radius of the curve will be respectively one-quarter or one-sixteenth part of that shown in the column against the Offset.

A table for the super-elevation on the outer rail of curves is given on the other side.

ENGINEER'S OFFICE,
WATERLOO STATION.   December, 1909.

rail (3'6") etc were all included. The book was regularly revised and the modern equivalent is still available doing the same job nearly 100 years later! Lastly, to pick one other aspect in this article which has evolved I will look at the loading-gauge profiles.

All three companies had developed strict loading gauge profiles. Of course some early tunnels infringed these standards, but all new work had to be to these standards. To this day there are still very tight clearances in some locations. Company officials would monitor these by measurement, including train-based measuring equipment from time to time, and special loads which were 'abnormal' would have to be checked against these profiles.

The minimum vertical structure gauge for the LSWR was 13'9", the LBSCR 14'0" and the SECR was 13'7". The Southern could not rebuild all to one standard, but all new work was constructed to 15'0" headroom and improvements made to existing structures where practical. Fortunately by the grouping all companies had adopted a standard platform height of 3'0", but horizontal clearances were slightly different for each pre-grouping company. Equally vehicle profile widths varied, the LSWR allowing an extra 3" to its stock width. All had different structure profiles so the SR quickly issued a standard profile to be adopted in future. Some structures such as tunnels were prohibitively expensive to alter so to this day there are tighter clearances on the LBSCR and even tighter ones on the old SECR such as the Hastings route. At least they all agreed on the track gauge! In the next article I will look at the development of standards for switch and crossing work.

References used:-

LSWR Switches and Crossings in the SW Circle literature April 2009 by Peter Bedding which contains a wealth of useful information.
Railway Permanent Way published in 1922. A full handbook of dimensional theory and practice.Hepworth and Thos. Lee.

LSWR Engineer's Department Tables.

Southern Railway Handbook. Instructions to Engineering. Department Staff 1929 and 1936.

The Circle Line. An Illustrated History, by Desmond Croome 2003.

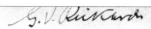

| L. S. W. R. | | ENGINEER'S DEPARTMENT. |

SPACING OF RAIL JOINTS.

The most careful attention must be paid to the spacing of rail joints, both in relaying and in the existing permanent way.

It is of great importance that correct spacing be preserved at all times.

As far as possible, the laying of new rails in the summer time should be undertaken early in the morning or during the after part of the day.

The rails must not be allowed to close up at the joints, nor be permitted to spread too far apart.

Directly spacing is found to be wrong, steps must be taken at once to adjust the rails.

As a guide to proper spacing the table hereunder is to be observed as closely as possible.

Condition of Weather.	Atmospheric Temperature at mid-day, approximately.	SPACES PER JOINT.	
	Degrees Fahrenheit.	Rails up to 30 feet long.	Rails above 30 feet and up to 45 feet long.
Hot (Summer) ...	About 90	3/32 inch.	5/32 inch.
Moderately Cool ...	,, 60	5/32 ,,	1/4 ,,
Cold (Winter) ...	,, 30	1/4 ,,	3/8 ,,

Inspectors, Foremen, and Gangers will be supplied with spacing gauges to assist them in conforming to the above instructions.

It is required that no effort shall be spared to keep all rail joints properly spaced.

ENGINEER'S OFFICE,
WATERLOO STATION,
October, 1904.

$(\frac{125}{64})$

MYSTERY PICTURE:

Obviously West of England but any ideas where? A wonderful assortment of p/way material visible in the foreground. Any ideas would be welcome.

BR Class 3MT No. 82023 in Waterloo dock on 28 January 1966.

Taken from "those flats" WC No. 34021 "Dartmoor" arrives at Waterloo with the 10 08 from Bournemouth West on 20 May 1965. The street in the background is Lower Marsh where I frequented some of the eating establishments every day before the regular evening visits down the line. Living in Kent I rarely ate at home for many years!

An engine I never travelled with WC No 34031 "Torrington" waiting to depart Waterloo with the 13 54 stopper to Basingstoke on 27 October 1964.

Confessions of a Steam Age Season Ticket Holder

extracts from a Waterloo commuters notebook

Keith Widdowson

Was it really 42 years ago last July when I arrived into Waterloo on that Sunday afternoon (the 9th) on the very last steam train into London - behind Merchant No. 35030 *Elder Dempster Lines*? I remember, after watching her depart light engine for Nine Elms, making my way, somewhat disconsolately, across the cab road, up the long connecting covered way, to the East station to catch my mundane 4-EPB slam-door suburban service to my North Kent home as if it was yesterday. Although it was over four decades ago I still remember feeling totally devastated at the loss of what had become such a passion, such an addiction, such a time-consuming hobby. For the previous three years all other 'requirements' such as work, relation visiting, family events, even eating, had been fitted in around the Waterloo-based steam services. Even when venturing to other parts of the country as one by one the surviving pockets of steam were eliminated there was always the knowledge that there would always be the Southern services to fall back on. Until then, that was. True, I could still travel north (albeit for a mere 13 more months) for weekend "fixes" of steam but what about the week nights? Although we enthusiasts all knew it was going to end one day, with typical teenage mentality that was always tomorrow and we would worry about that when it happened. Well, it had – and it was a sad and emotional time. For me and many other similar-minded friends that I had made it had become our way of life and unlike a great many teenagers it kept us off the streets and out of trouble (or none that our parents found out about!). Some of us 'blitzed' the Moorgate/Broad Street services (Class 23/24/25/31 diesels) or the Oxted line services (Class 33 diesels) in an attempt to occupy the weekday evenings now void of activity but the novelty soon passed.

There was no way of knowing that the renaissance of the Iron Horse, taken for granted by today's generation, was ever going to happen. Tourists or enthusiasts paying hundreds of pounds to travel behind preserved, resurrected, shiny, steam engines – dining on the best food – drinking the finest champagne – pull the other one! In 1967 the outlook was bleak. The main purpose of our hobby was being relentlessly taken from us. I wasn't to know that a quarter of a century later I was to be aboard the historic first return to a Southern London terminal of a steam-powered train (No. 34027 at London Bridge on 07 June 1992) and the NEXT steam departure from Waterloo (No. 34027 on 11 September 1992).

Returning to the final years of Southern steam - whilst appreciating the run-down condition and constant failures, such a frequent occurrence towards the end, I still feel privileged to have witnessed the scenario and participated in the chases with all their attendant emotional excitement and sadness. The Kinks pop group wrote their hit "Waterloo Sunset", perhaps based on the cessation of steam at Waterloo (or was that purely coincidental?) and even the national media (including those pirate radio stations moored outside British waters) gave some air space to the event. My small attaché case (16" x 10" x 4"), in regular use from January '66 to March '68, was stuffed full with my notebooks etc and filed away in my parents' attic. Luckily, having survived numerous domestic moves over time, it is now proving most valuable in rekindling memories sufficient enough for articles such as this to be compiled after all those intervening years.

During the final three years of steam operated commuter services out of Waterloo Keith Widdowson made over 350 return journeys to Woking, Basingstoke or Southampton. Graduating from a lunch time observer to a mileage bashing season ticket holder, he amassed more than 43,000 miles behind Bulleid's Pacific's. This is his story of Britain's final steam rush hour.

Where it all started

The first 3½ years of my career were based at the impressive General Manager's Offices at Waterloo. Perched high up on the fourth floor, panoramic views of London were available if looking North, with just a massive expanse of the glass-covered roof if looking south. In the summer you could sunbathe on the very top of the offices, next to the beehives and massive water tank which supplied the entire station's requirements but, with no railings and long drops all around, great care was needed. Although above the station roof you could still hear all the announcements and general noise emanating from the activities below – the major ones being the arrival (platforms 12-14) and departure (platforms 9-11) of steam-operated services. Not initially an enthusiast when joining British Railways, it was not until mid '63 that any interest in disappearing steam and line closures finally fired sufficient interest to propel me out to places I had often directed telephone callers to - in my job as telephone enquiry clerk. The 13.30 departure from Waterloo for Weymouth was often viewed from the end of platform 11 during my lunch break but with a greater amount of action on offer I sometimes travelled to/from Clapham Junction to view not just the Waterloo expresses but any yard activities and inter-regional freights. As a gopher (errand boy/office junior) I was sent all over Waterloo station – often having to descend into the labyrinth of archways and offices secreted in its bowels. For beneath Waterloo's concourse, away from the passages used by thousands of commuters hurrying along to either the Bakerloo/Northern lines or the 'Drain' to Bank, there were a myriad of establishments accessed through warm distillery-smelling passageways. One such underground thoroughfare was known as "The Long Valley", the main usage of which was the then extensive parcels traffic, off which there were side tunnels to the staff canteen, police offices and catering depots. At street level there was Lower Road with its range of arches containing parcel offices, lost property (staff could have their pick on Wednesdays from 12.00 to 13.00) and commercial offices where the region's closures notices were despatched from – one of each issue always falling into my hands! There were also commercial warehouses some of which contained alcohol from which the aforementioned smell came. During the Second World War a bomb set alight thousands of gallons of bonded spirits which burned so fiercely that the station was closed to all traffic for a week until the brickwork supporting the track above cooled down and was strengthened with temporary girders. A frequent collecting place for London's homeless population was Leake Street (a road running underneath the width of Waterloo station connecting York Way to the market in Lower Marsh), who were attracted there by the warm, cosy, dry environment where, at midnight, the Salvation Army's soup van made a regular visit. At the other end of the spectrum I was often sent to the plush carpeted top bosses' offices on the second floor, never actually seeing them but instead having to deal with their secretaries. Occasionally a visit to the station announcer's 'crows nest' was required of me from which a wonderful view of the entire station (from just under the roof) was obtained. For the best photographs of departing trains from Waterloo a block of high rise flats (Canterbury Rise?) near St. Thomas's hospital became a regular visiting point. Towards the end, however, the occupants became somewhat vociferous at the increasing numbers of us 'camping out' (being the days before secure/number-only entry) with photographic positions having to be relocated up or down a level depending on the ferocity of the complaints!

The office in which I worked also dealt with all the booking/reservations of Camping Coaches throughout the Southern Region and very popular they were too – the only condition of occupancy being that you had to

Waterloo on the 9th February 1965 and ex-SR U 2-6-0 No. 31639 makes a dramatic departure with the lightly loaded 13 54 departure for Basingstoke.

Over the weekends the Kenny Belle stock was stabled on the Windsor side of Clapham Junction to avoid vandalism (yes even in those days!) thus on Mondays starting from Platform 1. The remainder of the week, with the stock stabled behind the large advertising hoardings sandwiched between the Down Slow from Victoria and the Up West London Line, the normal departure platform was No 15. Photographed but not travelled on No. 82019 prepares for departure with the 08 16 service from Clapham Junction on Tuesday 7th June 1966.

travel by British Rail to/from your holiday. We made sure they did – we sold them the tickets! The complete list of locations escapes me but I do remember that some were located at Lyndhurst Road, Hinton Admiral, Sway and Wool. The vehicles themselves were redundant Pullman vehicles, gutted and made into living accommodation big enough to hold large families and whilst all on site problems/requirements could be dealt with by the resident station staff, the initial booking was at Waterloo. I well remember the busiest times were always Jan. – Mar. each year when everyone wanted to book the same school holiday weeks or public holiday weeks that summer (nothing new then!). We had a large board on the wall with the person's name on the required week/location on a yellow ticket – changed to blue upon receipt of their money. In November of `64 a static exhibition using one of the coaches was held at Waterloo and Victoria stations and I was proud to be selected as an assistant on board (I was only 17!) my duties being to distribute pamphlets and answer any questions the public asked. By then the increasing addiction to steam haulage was manifest within me and aware that, at Waterloo, the coach had to be shunted from the North Sidings to the main platforms (via West Crossings) sometime after the morning rush hour, I volunteered to travel on the shunt using the excuse that windows need to be opened and kettle switched on, etc. This proved a smart move, because for the three days the exhibition was on, the motive power was Standard Tanks Nos. 82013, 82023 and West Country No. 34103 *Calstock* – the latter two drivers giving me a footplate ride. Needless to say the Victoria shunt from Grosvenor sidings to the main station was with less interesting Class 33 or Class 71 locomotives.

Some years later I purchased a copy of the British Transport film "Terminus". Filmed in 1962 it depicts 24 hours in the life of Waterloo station and it is wonderfully accurate in its portrayal of every facet of life at a big London terminus and is <u>exactly</u> as I remem-

ber it – a happy workplace/force fondly remembered.

The railways, retrospectively, seemed to be stuck in a time warp. Everything went on as it always had done and always expected to but modernisation was on the horizon - the 1964 announcement of the Bournemouth line electrification spelling the end of steam traction being an obvious example. It stated that whilst the electrification from Pirbright Junction to Branksome was financially viable the remaining 32 miles to Weymouth was not, and that 19 Type 3 (Class 33) were to be converted to operate in push/pull mode for services over that section. The seemingly "insufficient funds" for complete electrification were "found" some 21 years later, thus highlighting the short sightedness always associated with money for any/every railway modernisation project - no change there then! In the immediate surroundings of SE1 changes were also happening with many photographs of steam at Waterloo station having the backdrop of the then futuristic Shell building – a concrete monstrosity still standing nowadays albeit a little weather-stained and having been converted into private accommodation. The Windsor line platforms, having dramatically altered the original neat overall appearance of the station to accommodate the lengthy Eurostar services, are now set to return to domestic use again. Of dubious notoriety is Waterloo's claim to accommodate Britain's longest automatic ticket barriers – are the vastly increased passenger numbers less honest than in the `60s?

Demise of the Maunsells

Initially wondering why I made notes of Maunsell, to the exclusion of Bulleid / Standard, engines seen whilst travelling on Waterloo steam journeys, I can only assume I must have realised that with the dieselisation of the Reading/Redhill route there was a vastly reduced amount of work (certainly passenger-service-wise) available for them and their numbers began to fall sig-

Freight shunting at Clapham Junction during one of my lunch time visits is U Class No. 31620. The date was 20 April 1964 and she survived for another 12 months.

nificantly. The 07.30 SX Woking to Basingstoke was booked for a 70C N Class but on the few occasions I saw/travelled on it a 73xxx was provided (i.e. No. 73037 on 26 March 1966) - the service going DMU in May `66. Another train booked for a 70C Mogul was the 15.12 Basingstoke to Woking stopper which, although often reported to have been worked by an S15, was, disappointingly, N No. 31858 when caught by myself on 07 August 1966. Sister engine No. 31873 worked the 19.54 Waterloo to Basingstoke on Wed 19 May 1965 which, had I not already travelled with her on the 09.43 Redhill to Guildford the previous year, I would have caught to Woking. By June `66 all the Maunsells had been withdrawn. I stupidly steered clear of railtours considering it a 'cheats' way (and expensive!) to obtain runs with steam locomotives, considering it much more rewarding to catch them on a normal service - this being all well and good if they ever did work normal services! The S15 class was a classic example of a missed opportunity, No. 30837, one of the last five examples withdrawn in September `65 was, however, kept in store for two LCGB railtours in January `66. In August 1965 I decided that if they weren't coming to me then I would go to them and Feltham shed was bashed - suitably accompanied by my faithful Kodacolour 35. I never did obtain a run with an S15 in service – a scenario subsequently corrected courtesy of The Mid Hants! The aforesaid failure changed my philosophy about railtours and starting with "The Wilts & Hants Railtour" in April `66, with N No. 31411 & U No. 31639 out of Waterloo, I travelled on a great many more!

Taking a general overview of ALL classes, 226 steam locomotives that were allocated to the SR made it into 1966, 130 into 1967 with a final withdrawal of 72 in July 1967. Classes of steam locomotives allocated uniquely to the Southern Region obviously became extinct from that date. Bulleid's West Country/Battle of Britain and Merchant Navy Pacifics together with the

USA tanks automatically qualify. Surprisingly so was the tank engine design itself – with examples elsewhere throughout Britain already having met with the cutter's torch – ex LMS Ivatt 2-6-2T, BR 2-6-4T and BR 2-6-2T became no more. With two other examples withdrawn the previous month elsewhere in Britain, the SR's only BR 3MT 2-6-0 No. 77014 also heralded the extinction of the class at a mere 13 years old!

The Kenny Belle

Kenny Belle was the nickname given to the unadvertised passenger service between Clapham Junction and Kensington (Olympia) - run for the benefit of workers at the nearby General Post Office headquarters. Not surprisingly it was used by a great many other members of the public – the need for such a service being vindicated by today's present day operators providing a regular all day interval service over the same tracks. Back in the `60s however, one 4-set (including the futuristic Lancing-built experimental fibre-glass reinforced plastic coach S10000) was deemed sufficient. Departures from Clapham Junction were 08.16 & 08.46 (EWD) returning from Kensington at 08.33(SX), 12.36 (SO), 16.36(MTX), 17.06(SX) or 17.36(MTO) – all services allocated to be worked by a Nine Elms tank locomotive. Just to confuse any intending traveller who didn't work for the Post Office days such as Maundy Thursday and Christmas Eve each year were treated as Saturdays and as such my first trip on the service was on the Thursday before Easter in 1965 with Standard 3MT 2-6-2T No. 82023 working the 12.36 departure. To get to Kensington (Olympia) for a southbound steam departure involved ascertaining if an exhibition (such as the Ideal Home) was being held in the nearby halls for which London Transport conveniently provided a District Line shuttle service from Earls Court – the alternative being a walk from Kensington High Street. An easier method was eventually discovered by boarding the outward empties from Clapham Junction – never having come across any problems after asking the guard and showing railway documentation to prove I was a railway employee! Indeed similar proof of railway employment often gained me access to all sorts of unorthodox movements Joe public would not have been allowed to embark upon! Being perhaps more interested in capturing runs behind Bulleids on the main line, I only travelled on the 17.06 or 17.36 services on 12 occasions during 1966, often catching runs with tank engines already travelled with during their previous allocations – particularly 75B & 83G. Afterwards I often attended the Rules and Signalling evening class held in a room above the platforms at Clapham Junction – which in turn enabled me to visit Wimbledon "A" box one evening in February `65. For a period of time (start date unknown) the services became Class 33 worked, returning to steam (my notebook states) from September `66.

Having left Waterloo in early `66 on promotion within the clerical grades to be a "journal marker" at DMO (SED) at Queen Street I subsequently moved to the Special Traffic section at DMO (SWD) at Wimbledon in the November of the same year. This meant that the journey from my Kent home to Wimbledon involved travelling via Victoria with another change at Clapham Junction and if and when services were running to time it meant that at Clapham Junction I was able to catch the 08.16 service to/from Kensington en route to work. I was therefore able to say that even though I lived in steam-starved Kent I too, like several of my work colleagues who travelled in from Farnborough/Woking, commuted to work on steam trains!

Although the morning service, for the final few months, was booked for a 70A 4MT, any tank available was provided. I made 62 journeys on the Kenny Belle behind 16 different tanks – Nos. 41284(1), 41298(1), 41312(2), 41319(4), 80012(1), 80015(3), 80085(7), 80089(1), 80133(2), 80140(4), 80143(1), 80145(6),

80154(1), 82019(18), 82023(1), & 82029(9) eventually accumulating 114 miles with No 82019 – anyone else out there obtain a greater mileage with a member of that class? I had thought the last Nine Elms tank I required was Ivatt No. 41284, eventually catching her on 9 February 1967, so a surprise, to me anyway, was the transfer in from Eastleigh of 'Mickey Tank' No. 41319. This was excellent for me because Eastleigh, by then, had no passenger work for their sole 2MT and there would have been little hope of catching her but now, sure enough, she eventually worked a Kenny Belle service I was able to catch – on 22 May 1967! She also had the dubious honour of working the last steam-operated morning service on Friday 7th July – which I was on.

Being unable to record the outward runs from Clapham because the train was very crowded, it was only the result of myself usually being the only passenger on the returning 08.33 service that I was able to document runs with drivers synonymous with main line exploits on this somewhat more mundane route though the West London suburbs. There were many speed restrictions along the 3¼ mile route - the fastest time I recorded was 7m. 1sec. with a maximum of 47mph between Pigeon S**t Bridge (Hither Green drivers' nickname for Chelsea Bridge which, in their opinion, was only held together by the said birds' excrement!) and Latchmere Junction. The highest speed I recorded was 51mph at West Brompton after an exhilarating departure from Olympia. Another bonus was the frequent sighting of one of London Transport's ex-GWR pannier locomotives at work in the Lillie Bridge area.

After steam finished the service was worked by a Class 33 – crewed during various periods from Waterloo, Hither Green or Norwood depots. I made one final trip on the service and that was on Friday 1 October 1982 when No. 33208 with a Norwood crew worked the last loco-operated service. After that date Redhill-crewed DMUs took over.

Light Pacific No 34017 "Ilfracombe" with the 13 30 departure on 03 November 1966. After lunching in the salaried staff canteen (adjacent to Platform 14), I often found myself viewing this departure - perhaps sowing the seed for my steam travels.

**In PART 2, Keith refers to speed runs behind steam, dieselisation and a few oddities.
Scheduled for Issue 10, April 2010.**

'M7' 30111 which features in the story, seen approaching Lymington Pier in the summer of 1951.

We are delighted to present the first in a series of articles from former Eastleigh Driver Hugh Abbinnett, on his experiences at some of the smaller sheds. Nowadays better known, years ago they were very much out of the way places and as a result life could be very different compared with the main line depots.

Tales from the Smaller Sheds

Hugh Abbinnett

Think of a loco shed and most people's immediate perspective will be something like Nine Elms, Eastleigh, Salisbury or Exmouth Junction: large, multi-road structures with perhaps ten to fifteen covered tracks plus all the requirements necessary to service and maintain the Southern Railway fleet of large and small engines. To those whose hobby was either photographing engines or collecting numbers, such places acted like the proverbial 'Mecca' as there was a guarantee that numerous engines would be seen, the individual then able to obtain his 'fix'.

But move away from the main line depot to more distant venues, and there were still sheds to be found. Nowadays amidst the plethora of published books available, their existence is perhaps well known, but years ago a branch line or secondary route could yield a surprise find, a home for perhaps one or two engines, smaller passenger or goods types, or even a place where a loco might be out-stationed so as to be ready for an early start. Sometimes too these sheds were the product of history, surviving long after a privately-owned line had been taken over and yet retaining a notional allocation, the engine ready to act swiftly in shunting wagons in a nearby yard or positioning goods ready for unloading. Time was when everything in the town or village was either produced locally or arrived by train. Those were the days before the supermarket, distribution centre and the adage 'big is beautiful' and 'small is inefficient'.

One of the sheds that came into this category and which was covered from my own depot at Eastleigh, was that of Lymington, at the end of a branch line which even years ago served a thriving local community as well as affording, via the connection with the main line at Brockenhurst, a connection for Waterloo suitable for the business classes. In addition the branch, for that is of course what it was, had a regular amount of traffic bound for the Island ferry, as during the season extra holiday makers arrived bound not just for the ferry but the nearby coastal resorts of the New Forest.

For many years, it was a pull-push member of the 'M7' class that was out-stationed at Lymington, the depot having, for some time at least, just two resident footplate staff, both drivers. These men worked opposite shifts but of course needed a fireman each, and it was then left to the socially inferior fireman to make his own way to the depot. But his task did not end there, for having undertaken some 20 five-minute trips to Brock-

enhurst and also shunted the yard at the Town station, it was not surprising that the bunker was by now a bit depleted of coal stock. Re-stocking was another duty for the fireman, achieved by a visit to the coal stack alongside the shed. A repeat procedure was needed on the late turn, added to which were cleaning and disposal duties so as to leave the loco in good condition ready for the early shift the next day. One particular fireman though, felt he might be able to save some of the evening work, so with his driver's blessing, he took the opportunity to cram every spare space there was on the footplate – and that was not a vast amount, with lumps of coal, large, small and, of course, the dreaded briquettes. Unfortunately the associated dust was not conducive to cleanliness and as the day wore on, so black dust invaded all parts of the footplate as well as the men upon it. The results can be imagined, even attracting unkind comment from some passengers.

It was not just mechanical preparation that was expected to be undertaken either: general cleanliness was also important, so by running that bit faster it was possible to gain a precious few minutes and thus have a little more time available for general cleaning; the fact passengers now had to endure a longer wait at the pier head for the ferry, or at Brockenhurst for their main line connection, was of little consequence.

As the ferries crossed in mid-stream, there was always going to be a wait at the Pier Station, the latter in effect a long siding, the end of which jutted out over the water. Here, alongside the platform, the M7 and its 2-coach (pull-push) set would quietly await the arrival of the incoming ferry, the Westinghouse pump slapping away, the fire damped down so as to keep the engine quiet and prevent the escape of steam. It was during this enforced wait, usually of around 20 minutes, that one day the fireman suddenly announced he was going for a swim. Having quickly changed into his trunks he plunged into the water, swimming strongly for the marker buoy that marked the mouth of the congested yachting area. At first the elderly driver appeared to condone the youngster's actions, but as the time for departure drew ever closer and there was no sign of the swimmer, so his anxiety grew. At this stage too the fireman was still on the outward stage of his swim but on hearing the call, 'Get back here nipper', he turned around and began his return leg to dry land and the footplate of No 30111. The driver meanwhile had already started to raise the boiler pressure by pushing the fire around the 'box. As they left for the run to Brockenhurst so the fireman was attempting a dual role, to dress himself as well as attending to his regular duties, the temperature on the footplate between the crew also being raised at the start. That at least had cooled by the time they arrived at the Town station, although at this stage the younger man still had not fully dressed himself: his trousers were still missing. Unfortunately the antics of wriggling legs back into blue serge were immediately noticed by passengers and staff alike and for a while at least he became the subject of much derision. Driver Curtis never ever allowed his fireman to go swimming again.

With only limited supervision on the spot, the crews would also work amongst themselves to make their tasks as easy as possible. This included bringing the relief firemen into the arrangement, provided they were both known and trusted. Accordingly, and to save everyone as much work as possible, the early turn fireman would arrive at the depot just as the late turn man was finishing off, blanketing down the fire with the intention of keeping the boiler warm but not enough to generate any steam. Equally important was to ensure the fire remained alight overnight! The early turn man would then ensconce himself comfortably in a First-Class compartment, taking with him an alarm clock. This would go off at the appointed time at which point it was just necessary to bring the engine round, before taking the engine on his own to the platform where the coaches were nicely warmed as well. All this had to be accomplished with the knowledge and consent of the resident drivers, making sure the driver's oiling was also already carried out. As such the driver could have some extra time in bed, the fireman saved himself a long cycle

ride on a cold morning, and the passengers arrived to a warm train. Of course this all depended upon the fireman arriving on time, so a scheme was devised whereby a particular tall lamp was switched on to indicate to the early turn driver all was well. Seeing the signal then the driver could simply turn over to enjoy that extra hour in bed. The equally well-prepared fireman would even have time for his own breakfast, cooked on the shovel, of course.

Problems though arose if a different man was on duty who did not know the arrangements, or if somewhere there was a lack of communication or understanding between parties. Then it was not just icy passengers in the mornings; the footplate itself could also become somewhat frosty.

Away from the footplate, the route of the line between the two destination stations passed through delightful New Forest heath land, at one point close by a farmhouse with paths leading down to the railway. Whilst in many ways an idyllic setting, the disadvantage was that it was impossible to have a daily paper delivered in the normal way. Here the branch drivers again came to the rescue, skilfully folding an old tabloid and by weighting it with stones at either end, they could successfully launch it from the window of the pull-push set and land it at the door of the farmhouse. The pending arrival of the news being identified by suitable shrieking of the whistle. This was successfully achieved 99 times out of 100, the only time it did go wrong when for some reason the driver's aim was poor and the package cracked the glass in the farmhouse door. Perhaps he had no need, but pride was at stake, so at the end of his shift that same driver arrived at the farmhouse complete with glass and putty intent on making good the damage.

End of the line at Lymington Pier, step back any further and it was into the water you go.

Anyone for a swim....?

A Coloured view of a Black & White era...

It is tempting to believe that everything illustrating the early years of railways, particularly the pre-grouping era, must of necessity be rendered in either black & white or sepia.

Technology which we nowadays take for granted was simply not available a century ago and as such it was to the artist that the railways turned to promote their message.

None was more involved in this area that the South Western, seen here through the covers of a wonderful collection of ephemera loaned to us by Michael Brooks.

Clearly one of the aims was to attract visitors to and from abroad, be that Europe , or as seen on this page, from further afield. Not surprisingly it is the covers which have the greatest appeal although once you were on board, economies seemed to apply - as witness the green and blue brochure opposite.

Later the Southern Railway would follow suit, although still perhaps with not quite the same obvious enthusiasm as the LSWR from years before.

London and

South Western Ry.

The Direct Route
from the **PORT OF PLYMOUTH** to
LONDON (Waterloo Station).

PLYMOUTH WATERLOO EXPRESS NEAR WILTON

Information

for Passengers Landing at the
Port of Plymouth from
Ocean Steamships.

DIRECT RAIL COMMUNICATION
BETWEEN THE
OCEAN QUAY STATION
AND
London (Waterloo Station) and all parts
of Great Britain.

CHAS. J. OWENS, General Manager.

THIS YEAR COME TO ENGLAND

BY CUNARD LINE

With compliments of the
SOUTHERN RAILWAY
OF — ENGLAND

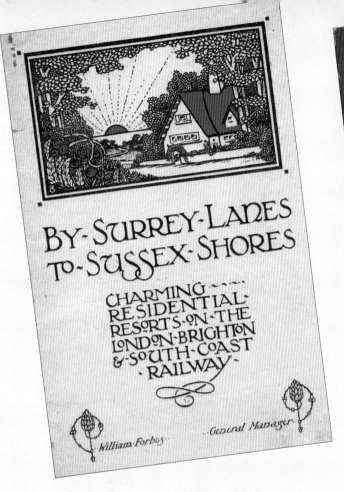

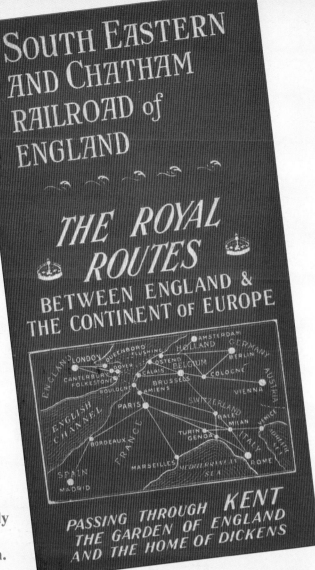

Contemporary material from the other Southern constituents, these examples perhaps slightly
bland by comparison but still attractive none-
theless.   Michael Brooks collection.